PENGUIN BOOKS
ELSEWHERE

Kai Friese edited the *India Magazine* from 1995 until 1998. He is currently Features Editor of *M̶·̶·̶¹̶ ̶W̶·̶·̶¹̶*

...magazine

elsewhere

unusual takes on India

Edited by Kai Friese

PENGUIN BOOKS

Penguin Books India (P) Ltd., 11, Community Centre, Panchsheel Park, New Delhi-110 017, India
Penguin Books Ltd., 27 Wrights Lane, London W8 5TZ, UK
Penguin Putnam Inc., 375 Hudson Street, New York, NY 10014, USA
Penguin Books Australia Ltd., Ringwood, Victoria, Australia
Penguin Books Canada Ltd., 10 Alcorn Avenue, Suite 300, Toronto, Ontario, M4V 3B2, Canada
Penguin Books (NZ) Ltd., Cnr Rosedale and Airborne Roads, Albany, Auckland, New Zealand

First published by Penguin Books India 2000

This anthology copyright © Penguin Books India 2000
Introduction copyright © Kai Friese 2000

Copyright for the individual essays rests with the respective contributors

All rights reserved

10 9 8 7 6 5 4 3 2 1

Typeset in Bembo by Eleven Arts, Delhi-110035

Printed at Thomson Press, New Delhi

Contents

Introduction

This collection of non-fiction writing consists of twenty articles that appeared in a magazine I edited between 1995 and 1999. I'm delighted to see them in print again for a variety of reasons, but when I began work at the *India Magazine* (the *India Magazine of Her People and Culture*, as sniggering cognoscenti will recall) I had rather mixed feelings. The downside: it was a boring magazine, an interminable loop of features on that 'timeless' India intended for people who spend their air-conditioned lives padding across the coir matting between the divan and the coffee table. Ganjifa Cards, Toda Tales, Dances with Gonds.

That kind of thing. The upside was that the entire editorial team had quit minutes after we were introduced. 'Perhaps you can make it a bit more contemporary,' said my new employers. It would have been difficult to do anything else.

Over the next few years, by the simple expedient of harassing literarily inclined friends and acquaintances up to about four degrees of separation, the *India Magazine* became arguably the most readable Indian magazine you've never read. Looking through this collection I'm surprised we got so much from so many for so little. But these were the last quiet days before the hype, and many of the writers you might now recognize were still trying to make an honest living. They were filmmakers, academics, editors, 'consultants' and what have you. It made for an eclectic mix which had the grain of daily life, its pleasures and perils. It was not as one long-time subscriber complained, 'the great golden *India Magazine* of yore'. Yes, it was pretty contemporary.

Now it's history—the victim of the publisher's sudden enthusiasm for economy. First they stopped paying our contributors—no problem, they kept writing. Then they stopped paying salaries—no problem, we kept coming to work. Emboldened by the success of these two cost-cutting measures, they finally stopped paying the paper suppliers and the printers as well. After that they seemed fairly pleased and pretty much left us alone.

I spent a year in this dreamlike state, editing a magazine that would never be printed, earning a respectable salary that I would never receive. However it was a learning experience. When you spend a year responding to the salutation 'Bastard, where's my cheque?' you learn to pass the buck. So to speak. It is customary at this point to make a few exculpatory remarks about your associates and utter provisional mea culpas for your own trespasses. I'd rather not.

So thanks: to Mohana, Nikhil, Sid, Roma, Latha, Shukha, and Naga, ex of the *India Magazine*. And to Anjana and Bena at Penguin India.

Obviously, I did not write this book. I don't recall editing it either, beyond passing a few photocopies of my favourite articles to the publishers. Of course I'm very glad it happened. But the responsibility lies, well, *Elsewhere*.

AMIT CHAUDHURI

The House on Debendra
Ghose Road

It has already begun to fade from my memory. At first it was an assignment, an agreement on a bad telephone line, something to be done, a commitment. Then a contact was made.

It was an old, stately mansion near Jagu Bazaar, where I arrived on a hot morning in April. I asked for directions to the lane, Debendra Ghose Road, and once there, asked, at a *bidi* shop, for directions to the house; the man pointed towards it. He seemed to take for granted the presence of an old house on the street, as if he took time and fortune's discrepancies for granted, or as if his world were too full for him to be preoccupied with a man asking for directions.

I came to the gates and saw the house, for the first time, from the outside; it was unrecognizable—even a 'decaying house' does not approximate the image you already have of it. I asked the *dhoti-clad* man at the steps for the gentleman I was to meet. 'Oh. He'll be in soon. Or he could already be here. Upstairs.' The man had the relaxed air of the family retainer. Someone who has belonged to a house for so long that it has almost come to belong to him, without the constricting and poignant burden of ownership. I walked up the stairs, confronted a large mirror, and then climbed up another flight of stairs. Two men in bush shirts were huddled around a table on a marble verandah. One was scribbling away on a piece of paper; the other would consult the piece of paper occasionally. The table before them had a marble top and wrought-iron legs. There was a vague resemblance between them, which I took to be features shared in common by people who belonged to the same generation and community. I thought they might be relatives of the gentleman I was to meet; they were endearing and polite, telling me that he would be along soon, and inviting me to sit down and have a cup of tea.

As it turned out, the men were descendants of the barrister who had bought this house in the nineteenth century— Debendra Ghose, after whom the lane was named. One of the gentlemen handed me, as I was drinking tea, the scrap of ruled paper he had been writing on. 'All the history', he said, smiling as he transferred the scrap of paper to me, 'is in there.' I have since misplaced that scrap of paper or, at any rate, put it inside some drawer. I still have with me, however, the taste of the *sandesh* and other sweets that were bought, no doubt, from a sweet-shop nearby, and which we all ate later.

Fifteen more minutes were spent on that island of marble, an old fan above our heads, the morning arrested outside, and wooden railings enclosing us. There was a wooden partition to my right, on which the caretaker had pasted a gallery of calendar pictures of gods and goddesses.

Once Mr Ghose, whom I'd been waiting for, arrived, the four of us set out to explore the first storey of the mansion, a gentle and enthusiastic commentary accompanying me on all sides. We first entered the bedroom, uncarpeted (as large houses used to be), the stone floor shining with indirectly reflected light, photographs on the wall, and a double bed on the far side of the room, where, if I recall correctly, a few photographs and books had been placed against the bolsters and the white bedcover. The last occupant of this room had been Mr Ghose's aunt, a widow, and since widows used to wear white, one could almost see her outline merging with the white bedcover. I was told that a man in one of the photographs, one end of his *dhoti* partly faded out of existence, was Girindrashekhar Bose, brother of the great short-story writer, Rajshekhar Bose, and related to this family by marriage. 'That's extraordinary,' I said. 'Just the other day I was reading an essay about him by Ashis Nandy: he was the first non-Western psychoanalyst, wasn't he?' There were grave and delighted nods, and a polite query regarding the author of the essay. Who was this man writing about a family member who, albeit an exotic specimen, they thought had been forgotten? The essay had spoken of a correspondence with Freud, the setting up of the first society of psychoanalysts in India, the teaching of the discipline at the university and a childhood spent learning magic tricks—it was such beginnings that led to the earliest gentle delvings into that virgin, uncharted world, the Indian, the Bengali, psyche. And here he was, on this hot morning, in this photograph.

I was then led out of the room into the long verandah at the rear, which looked out on a courtyard, on another part of the house now rented out, and, further away, on a relatively 'new' annexe, where I was told the two gentlemen who had been waiting for me lived with their families. Meanwhile, this house, originally bought from someone else by Debendra Ghose, continued to lead its own life, to decay, to receive visitors; and it was strange how the old joint family, dead or dispersed now, gravitated to this source, architecturally or otherwise, living in adjoining annexes, or returning to it, as I was informed, during the Pujas and the festivals.

The first floor (in contrast to the ground floor, where the barrister would meet his clients and colleagues and consult his texts) was the arena of privileged domesticity and sexuality, defined by the bedroom, the cool stone floor where children might lie and play, and the dressing room on the extreme right, where adults changed before going out. My companions recalled how the family had been an early proponent of widow marriage, and that a widowed daughter had been actually remarried, a radical move in its time. Amazement and pride about that act still survived in the present retelling. The repercussions of such changes would have been principally, and fundamentally, felt here, on the first floor, with its self-concealing, self-discovering arrangement of corridors, rooms, furniture and doorways.

The photographer arrived, perspiring, later than expected— he'd been detained, not surprisingly, by a traffic jam in the north. The three gentlemen, endlessly accommodating, gave us another short tour of the house, the photographer considering angles and views, and I conferring with him about the pictures I might like him to take. I was already trying to hoard away details, facts; when first coming in, I had been struck in particular by a crack on the marble doorstep at the entrance, a triangular absence that seemed to signify, as rings do on bark, or as a frayed patch does on a coat, the attrition of life and memory upon a material thing, the wear and tear of a thing's usability. But it was not an ancient crack; it had been made the previous week, when a workman had dropped something heavy on the step; the chipped piece of marble had been laid to rest in the corridor. The crack, I was delighted to discover, was the only really new thing in the house.

Not much later, we left, and returned to the heat outside. A month passed, and, in the most natural of processes, I began to forget the house, the details I had thought I would memorize, the exact location of objects, its wings and antechambers and rooms. It was then that I began to want to write about it; not only to describe the house or its history, but to enter the space in which it had been temporarily forgotten, and from which it might be recovered.

(August/September 1996)

SHUDDHABRATA SENGUPTA

Long Distance Conversations

I am a prisoner of phone booths. STD/ISD/PCO/FAX/XEROX by Japanese machine, booths. I am enthralled by their darkened glass panes, stencilled signage and plastic flowers, the late hours they keep, and the stories that gather on their wallpapers. Like an idiot hungry for tales of travellers who idled in the serais of the Delhi sultanate, I waste my time in the phone booths of 90s New Delhi. Even when I have nothing to say and no one to call.

An STD phone booth is like a caravanserai, where you can alight at odd hours from the journeys of everyday life and hear news of distant places. The phone booths close to where I live host Afghan refugees and Israeli backpackers, Malayali nurses and Gujarati traders in transit. I go there to sit next to travellers and people with faraway relatives, and to listen to strange languages being spoken. I go there to eavesdrop on the world, because the world inhabits phone booths. I go there to whisper in my head the magic of distant place names—Adas, Addagadde and Ahwa, Galagali, Galsi and Gambhoi, Kanjirapuzha, Kalna and Kantilo, Zira, Ziro and Zineboto. Or, I search farther in the book of codes for cities with enchantments—Rosario, Erevan, Chittagong, Oruru, Tenerife, Uppsala, Valparaiso, Leipzig,

Hafnart-Joerdur, Zauqa, Dewaniya, Sabh, Sert and Yundum . . . and Aqaba . . . and Sandnes . . . and Los Angeles.

A single operation of the fingers, and I could be talking to someone I do not know in Rosario, Argentina. A phone would ring, somewhere in the world, someone would pick it up at another hour, in another hemisphere, perhaps on the following or in the previous day, in another season, and ask who is calling in another language.

As some people collect views of other places in postcards, to remind themselves of places they can only dream of, would someone begin a collection of recordings made over the phone of surprised voices in other languages? Would they play these recordings to themselves late at night on a *barsati* terrace? Would there be exhaustion, laughter, irritation and sorrow in those voices? Would there be rudimentary, crude, grunting conversations: found sounds, like found images, scattered and then gathered between time zones in the phone booths of New Delhi?

All this is possible in a New Delhi phone booth. But there are other, more serious purposes that justify their ubiquity. Business, family, marriage, news of sudden death, examination results, birthday greetings and homesickness. Love, real estate, births, exports. Arrivals and departures, the distress of stranded tourists, illness and the stock market.

In the course of an hour and a half waiting for a clear line to Bombay I hear snatches of all this. I hear of broken engagements and faulty diagnoses, of mothers-in-law and travel agents, of missed opportunities and the daily grind. I hear the trivial details of everyday lives compressed to save time, and money.

STD booths heal. They purge us of the dross of our lives by allowing us to jump time and distance and have our say to that faraway person who is suddenly so important. They cripple us, because letters lie unwritten in our drawer, and 'I'm all right. Are you OK. Call next week' becomes a catch-all substitute for conversation. They perform miracles, because, like the little boy who walks out of the booth and asks his father why it's afternoon there when it's night over here, I still can't quite believe that I can speak to someone in their yesterday.

There are thousands of phone booths in a city like Delhi, and their number grows exponentially. As they thrive, they replace barber shops, grocery stores and milk queues as the hubs of conversation and social life in a neighbourhood. Gradually, each booth builds up a clique of regulars, nodding acquaintances to each other, but well aware of the intricate details of each other's family histories. This tends to happen because it is impossible not to have a fair idea of what people are saying in a phone booth. The most private conversations become public when they are long distance. People still tend to shout down the phone line, both because the lines are bad and because the act of speech traversing the distance, say from Lajpat Nagar to Dhanbad, still seems by consensus to require greater volume, intensity and projective power.

Phone booths also become centres of night life, venues for illicit assignations and coy flirtations between students and singles living in one-room sets. I have seen a love affair form and then conduct itself, ever since both its protagonists met at a booth. One travelled to a distant city, and many long phone calls later, betrayed the other, who continued to call long distance from the same phone booth to berate her unfaithful, 'has been' lover.

Each phone booth has a distinct character, which consists of an amalgam of the people who manage it and its repertoire of clients.

Thus, there are little holes in the wall which are proof of a *panwallah's* sharp business acumen. Salesmen and commercial travellers gather here for a late-night cigarette and have abbreviated conversations about money, with their out-of-town partners. Then they call up their wives, perfunctorily.

There are phone booths run by auntyjis that cater to a family audience, men and women in night dresses and children come here to talk at length to relatives in the course of an after-dinner stroll. Their conversations are lively and encompass a universe that stretches from infidelity to toilet training.

Hi-tech booths with fax machines and the beginnings of E-mail are the arena for the urban professionals, who can't get rid of their mobile phones even when surrounded by so many other kinds of telephones. These are efficient but unfriendly places manned by sharp-looking young men. Even late into the night, in the quarter-charge hours, this crowd makes it a point to be well dressed, and a little anxious to be noticed. Here the operators and bosses sit behind an array of the latest in telephony. They transfer calls, coordinate conferences between five different callers and exude the kind of power that is associated with priests, magicians and orchestra conductors.

There are STD booths that offer xerox facilities, which are favoured by university students. They come to ask their parents in their home towns for money and to get their lecture notes and texts photocopied. These are malnourished and often lonely people. Their eyes red with sleeplessness and worries about exams, careers, the rent and impossible love affairs. They often stand still after their conversations and ask for credit, or painfully part with their very little money. They leave the phone booth just as they came, embarrassed and forlorn.

Then there are dingy and suspect premises hidden in the basements of commercial complexes. These see little activity, barring unsuspecting tourists trying to call Jerusalem, or Amsterdam. The real players here are the owners themselves, the men who sit behind unused telephones and wear dark glasses even when indoors and surround themselves with the musty smell of cheap incense. They crowd their walls with images of the Sai Baba of Shirdi and 'Jai Mata Di' stickers. On hot summer afternoons, when no one ventures out to make STD calls, they dial in to Indore, Bulandshahar, Cuttack and Mogulsarai and rapidly read out a list of numerals—5, 9, 3, 43, 17 ... Those are the conduits of the *satta* trade, relayers of the day's lucky digits to number-gambling cartels spread across the underbelly of small town India. When approached to make a phone call they will often tell you with an implacable, greasy and mysterious smile that the lines are out of order.

Phone booths in the city centre, close to railway stations and cheap hotels, are home to a floating population of tourists and travellers in various stages of fatigue and enthusiasm. As they unbuckle their voluminous rucksacks and unzip their hip pouches to take out scraps of paper with phone numbers in Belgium or Germany, they can be seen imagining the prospects of return and mapping their future itineraries—will it be Ladakh before Goa, or Dharamshala before Benares? These are the roving envoys of the lonely planet, fixing their next destination well in advance, enquiring after jobs left behind, and desperately trying to make friends as they wait their turn. They are invariably overcharged by smooth phone booth owners who hide their racism behind the complicated arithmetic of time and money conversions.

Despite the inherent variety of the people in them, the phone booths have certain common architectural features. A big yellow sign with a red arrow across the street. Plastic bucket chairs, a calendar image of Shiva or Ram astride the would-be temple at Ayodhya, a statuette of Ganesh or the Virgin Mary, a framed print of a fat baby reading the holy Quran, wallpaper, formica tables, aluminium and glass partitions, second-hand air conditioners, plastic flowers and a black-and-white television set at an elevation.

Sometimes on the wall behind the manager there is a film star's portrait, or large poster of alpine Switzerland, and a set of clocks with the hands showing different hours, each neatly labelled with legends saying UK (London), USA (east coast and west coast), GERMANY, NEW DELHI, TOKYO, MOSCOW (Russia) and GULF. The decor of phone booths suggests an imagination that brings together sections of airports, the kitsch of drawing rooms and the aspirations of the office premises of a small business— domesticity, the world abroad and the trappings of efficiency.

The phone booth negotiates between these, and simultaneously between nostalgia, the desire for a better, more glamorous life and a Protestant ethic sternly spelt out in notices in bold type.

'Be Brief—Time is Money—Work is Worship.'

'Wrong numbers dialled will be strictly charged for.'

'Management is irresponsible for line failure or engage tone.'

'Make no love talk here—others are in queue.'

Yet, no matter how many guides to STD etiquette get pasted on to the space next to Shah Rukh Khan's smile on a phone booth wall, the random and unpredictable quality of phone booth behaviour cannot be contained.

A group of Malayali nurses, exceptionally graceful, who answer to the names of Minnimol, Gracekutty and Malathi regularly call up family in their home town Kalamassery. They ask after nephews and the price of coconuts, sometimes are worried by the fact that the money order sent for Easter hasn't reached, or that a cousin has eloped.

Every week on the appointed day, after their calls are made and the change is tendered, the boss of our phone booth asks them searching questions about the Christian faith. Is the holy ghost a ghost? Was Jesus reborn after his death? Did the Virgin Mary have a normal delivery? Do Christians have caste?

Painstakingly the Malayali sisters answer these queries in halting Hindi. Sometimes they promise to find out from the priest and clarify a difficult issue. Once they leave, the boss shakes his head solemnly. These exchanges are not brief. The boss doesn't charge them for wrong numbers and he lets them jump the queue. No one seems to mind. Not even the anxious exporter who makes a scene if any one else redials a number. Minnimol, Gracekutty and Malathi are the familiars of our booth.

When I can't get through to a friend in a city that was once called Bombay, or I get too much interference on the line to Frankfurt, Munich or Sydney, I think of Minnimol's patient exhortation, 'Just try again, simply one more time only', and sometimes it works. Or at least we all like to think it does.

Not everyone comes away from our phone booth contented. Raminder Kaur breaks down every time she speaks to her son in Vancouver. Her husband, who escorts her out, is always smug. He never speaks, though he helps her dial the long and complicated code number. Each time she makes a collect call, and each time her son disconnects at the other end, and each time she gets hysterical she begs us all to help her dial again. But her husband cajoles her out of the booth and takes her back into the unhappiness she comes from.

A medical representative stops by on his way after a long shift on Wednesdays and Fridays. He deals in drugs for psychiatric ailments, and I have seen him pass strips of pills quietly to Raminder Kaur's husband. Each time he dials a number in Bangalore, he takes out a letter and says something furtively into the phone. Then he steps out of the aluminium and glass cabinet and sits quietly in a corner of the booth, staring at his polished shoes, or carefully examining his fingers. After all the calls are nearly over, at 12:40 or so, there's just me, a backpacker still trying to get through to Barcelona, and the boss, who is watching cable TV. The phone rings, and the dealer in pills for unhappiness rushes in, unloosens his tie and asks, 'Husband is asleep?'

The boss and the backpacker are asleep as well by now, and for the next twenty-five minutes the shiny-shoed salesman makes long-distance love to a married woman in Bangalore. Sometimes he breaks off from Kannada, and begins talking about her long hair in English. The peculiar, furtive melancholy of his voice is perhaps the only consolation that she has ever had, and till ten past one on Wednesdays and Fridays he sings her his song. He remembers their days together, promises to write, tells her about Delhi, and about how the mental hospital here is nothing compared to the one in Bangalore. He asks for news of her children, jokes about the sleeping husband, and promises to see her soon. In the end he whispers to her things that are perhaps too intimate to speak out aloud.

The backpacker is awake by now and impatient again, and he wakes up the boss. The drug salesman finishes his call and before leaving offers me some *pan masala*. The backpacker calls Barcelona and he can't get through. I try calling a friend in Germany and I can't get through either. The boss begins counting the day's takings. One thousand and twenty-seven rupees. Then he begins rolling down the shutter.

The boss of my neighbourhood phone booth is a generous quasi-insomniac, but even he locks up his business at one o'clock. The booths that claim to provide twenty-four hours service actually stay open only till midnight.

There are very few places you can go to at the dead of night to call. I offer to drive the backpacker down to the all-night STD phone outside the Eastern Court buildings on Janpath. I still have to make my call, and so does he. We drive in silence, we have things to say to the people we have to call, not to each other. Then my companion decides to tell me that his friend is dead and cold in a hospital morgue, that he is catching the next flight back in the morning with her body. He lapses into silence. When we get there, he lets me wake up the operator and get the cards with which to work the phones. He shuts the door tight behind him when he calls, and I cannot hear his voice. When he is done, he thanks me and leaves before I can ask him if I can take him to his hotel, or to the hospital. As I dial I can hear a taxi go away into the night.

A phone call is measured in terms of time and money in red liquid crystal display digits that glow in the dark like malformed fireflies. The backpacker's call to Barcelona that night was brief and it cost him three hundred and fifteen rupees. He never bothered to pick up his receipt when he left. How did he say what he had to tell his friend's family? 'Flavia and I are coming home tomorrow, but she is not alive', or 'Flavia died this morning at six-forty-five in her sleep', or just, 'Flavia is dead.'

A phone call breaks the pattern of an evening in a Barcelona home. Sudden distant death intrudes upon a family sitting down to supper. They make more phone calls, arrange for the funeral, find a picture of Flavia taken just before she had left for India and send it to the photographers for enlargement and framing.

They wait, and so does the backpacker, and the time and distance involved in the transit of the body make it difficult to mourn. Death, Flavia's particular death, takes on an unreal, virtual mantle, existing only in a phone call made at midnight in the Eastern Court phone booth.

An Afghan doctor and his wife, recent refugees from a meaningless and forgotten war, come to a phone booth I know to ring up Kabul. I asked them once whether they still have friends or relations there. 'No', they said, 'every one dead, or in exile. We call only to see if the house we left behind is still standing. When the phone rings, it means that the house has not been shelled.'

A phone that no one attends to in a vacant house that waits to be shelled.

A phone call that's made in which nothing is said.

A phone call that isn't made because the person is too close at hand.

All the conversations in the world are made in part of silence. And sometimes the silence overshadows the rest. It becomes possible to talk at, past or around someone, without really speaking to them. For a long time now, I have needed to speak with a friend I meet every day, or every other day. We talk about work, schedules, the books we've read and the films we have been sitting through, we do not talk about ourselves.

At these times I feel the need to make a long distance call to this person close at hand. Perhaps the need to say a great deal in too short a time would act as a necessary prelude to a real dialogue, pursued at length and with leisure.

How far would I have to travel from the city that we inhabit for this to happen? Would Meerut be far enough, would Port Blair be the right distance, would I get through from Calcutta, or from Goa? Would I need to travel to the other end of the world, to Rosario or Buenos Aires in Argentina? Would I need to be in winter when it is summer here, or in night in place of day? And would it do then to just say hello, or would we have to cajole a conversation out of its hiding places? Would we just find things to say that fall in place, naturally, yet still as if by magic?

Sometimes I think of all the telephone conversations that criss-cross the earth and all the things that still remain unsaid. Numbers don't match, there is static interference, satellite links fail and even when people get through they don't know what to say, or are unable to say what they mean. Perhaps all that is unsaid collects each night and hovers above us like an unknown layer in the atmosphere until it is blown away on the rare days when people find it possible to really speak to each other. Those are the days on which the STD booths shine, their tin and paint banners gleam as if washed in a new rain. And the quiet hum of phone lines and many ringing dial tones signal the everyday fact of people enjoying the things they have to say to each other, across real and imagined distances.

(August/September 1996)

P. SAINATH

The Elephant Man

There was no mistake about it. It was an elephant out there. With a man sitting on top of it. We were walking along a deserted stretch on the Sarguja-Palamau border when we first saw man and beast. At least we thought we had. The three of us checked this out with each other. We were not, however, in a hurry to go and check it out up close.

It annoyed Dalip Kumar, who had come down from Chandwa to meet me. Our attitude, he pointed out, was absurd. 'If we saw the same sight in Patna or Ranchi or any other town, we would not think it odd at all. This is jungle. Elephants belong here. And we are being stupid.'

Maybe that's why we were being stupid. This was jungle. Dalip was being perfectly logical, of course. But he confessed to a marked lack of enthusiasm himself when it came to following up logic with action. Besides, for a while, we were not sure we had really seen a man on top.

By this time, though, the man had seen us. He waved out cheerfully and steered his huge vehicle in our direction. Her name was Parbati and she was as gentle a soul as you could meet anywhere. His own name, fittingly, was Parbhu. He was taking her to a temple in some place we had never heard of. They made the rounds of all the temples in the area, he explained. There they could earn some money. More if there was a festival on. Also, the good people of the villages en route gave them a bit of food and money.

Parbhu said he stayed in Sarguja in Madhya Pradesh. But he and Parbati moved about on both sides of the border with Palamau. The single district of Sarguja is larger than the states of Delhi, Goa and Nagaland combined. Palamau belongs to Bihar. Both are among the very poorest districts in the country. That is, they have very large numbers of poor people. In terms of resources, both are fabulously rich.

Parbati is probably of distinguished lineage. The elephants of Sarguja were famous in history for their crucial role in battle. As the district gazetteer puts it: 'In medieval warfare, elephants were the most important source of strength. Hence the Sarguja state of Chattisgarh was one of the important centres from where elephants were procured during that period. The relationship of the Sultans of Malwa with the rulers of Sarguja was calculated on this basis: that they assured Malwa of a constant supply of elephants.'

Malwa, in fact, considered this the most important reason for retaining its suzerainty over Sarguja. It was hard, though, looking at them, to visualize the ancestors of Parbhu and Parbati as fierce and warlike. Parbhu seems the soul of docility. And Parbati looks about as warlike as a rabbit (if you can imagine a very, very large, peaceful rabbit).

Dalip, the driver of the ancient jeep we had hired in Ambikapur and I had been searching for a village we finally never found. We had parked the jeep near a small Birhor colony. The Birhors are a very ancient tribe. They are of the same Austro-Asiatic language group as the Ho, Santhal and Munda tribes. A nomadic tribe of the Chottanagpur belt, they move mainly around Palamau, Ranchi, Johardaga, Hazaribagh and Singhbhum. They are a vanishing people. There are just around 2,000 of them in all today, perhaps less.

This clan of Birhors had told us of an interesting village that they said was 'nearby'. We were now in the process of learning that it is fatal to accept a nomadic person's understanding of 'nearby'. We had left the jeep, which had been giving us trouble, in the care of the Birhor and gone ahead on foot.

The driver wanted to go with us. He was scared of the way the Birhors looked, he said. Now he was scared of the way Parbati looked. Dalip made some terse remarks on how he thought the driver looked, but the man went with us just the same.

Parbhu generously offered us a ride. We accepted. I had been counting the number of different forms of transport I had used since I set out on my project months ago. They ranged from country boat and raft to the tops of trains. An elephant was not on the list. Some distance down the trail, we sat down to talk to Parbhu. We wanted to know how he fed and maintained Parbati.

All our interviewing skills proved useless. An hour and a half later we had learnt precisely nothing. Parbhu was sweet but cagey. He said they lived okay, off the alms they got from people and at temple fairs. In some parts of the country that would be true. Here it could not be. 'You . . . liar,' said Dalip. 'That thing needs 200 kg of grass. Plus other food. I'll tell you what you do. You let her forage in the cultivated fields nearby, don't you?'

This was probably true. Parbhu denied it flatly. 'We may as well interview the bloody elephant,' said Dalip. 'She'd be more truthful. He can't get too deep into the forests to feed her. There are real wild elephants up there. And other creatures. No, he loots the fields. He just takes her out there and lets her devastate the crop.' As we discussed her diet and bills, Parbati kept playing with Parbhu, her trunk running over his head. That she loved him was clear. If he looted the fields, he did a good job of it.

There were times, said Parbhu, when *bade log* hired their services. For instance, a Parbati dressed up in finery made a grand spectacle at a wedding. The last one they graced, though, was not quite so profitable. 'The *malik* cut fifty rupees from the total,' said

Prabhu. 'Parbati had been hungry that day. And she helped herself to some of the food there when she shouldn't have.' He slapped her lightly on the trunk. Maybe remembering the loss of the fifty rupees. She wheezed affectionately. Maybe remembering the meal at the wedding.

'Once a man came and said he wanted to hire Parbati for a procession. His leader was contesting an election. But it didn't happen. He said later that some people had told him bad things about Parbati. That she was not reliable. People do these things,' he said sadly.

Didn't he have problems when he entered villages where the sight of Parbati created much excitement? 'Once', said Parbhu, 'a whole lot of dogs started barking at Parbati and snapping at her. She got scared and tried to retreat. She backed into a house and there was some damage. The owner of the house was very angry.'

We speculated in silence for some moments. What was it like to be owner of a house that Parbati backed into? What must the house look like after the event? Was the owner very angry or just terrified to death?

'Another time', said Prabhu, 'people threw stones at Parbati outside a village.'

'Ah!' said Dalip triumphantly. 'That must have been when you were looting the fields.'

'No, no. We were just passing through their fields. I think some of the men were drunk. They threw stones. We retreated in another direction. Unfortunately, it was getting dark. And there was another *basti* there that we entered. And Parbati was moving quickly. So people there got frightened. She was not being aggressive at all. They just panicked needlessly and started screaming.'

We wondered what we would do if a huge elephant charged into our midst out of the darkness. Maybe we wouldn't throw stones at it. But panic and screaming seemed pretty much on the agenda.

The more we looked at it, the more complex the problem of Parbhu and Parbati seemed. The overwhelming majority of Sarguja's human beings do not eat properly. How then, to feed an elephant? Or was Parbati feeding Parbhu by way of the earnings she brought in?

Apart from elephants, Sarguja has historically been famous (or infamous) for its poverty. The Sultanate, the Mughals, the Marathas and the British all levied their lowest taxes or tributes on this state. The Sultans and Mughals mostly settled for elephants. As late as 1919, the British, who were extracting fortunes from neighbouring states, were settling for a pittance here. Each year they took just Rs 2,500, Rs 500 and Rs 387 respectively from the local feudatory states of Sarguja, Korea and Chang Bhakhar.

In the last years of the eighteenth century, the Marathas overran the feudatory state of Korea, then under Sarguja's suzerainty. Even the mighty Marathas could not take full possession of the territory—finding it too difficult a terrain to control. Instead, they demanded a mere Rs 2,000 from the Raja of Korea. Discovering that he could not pay, they lowered this charge to Rs 200 a year for five years and grabbed several head of cattle in warning. Soon, according to the district gazetteer, even the ruthless Marathas came around to understanding that the Raja could not pay a single rupee. They settled, therefore, for 'five small horses, three bullocks and one female buffalo'.

Then they released and even returned some of the other cattle they had looted, finding them largely worthless. The hostilities came to an end and the Marathas marched back.

So how does one feed an elephant in Sarguja? One that you can't take too deep into the forest? We were no nearer to an answer than we had been earlier. One last, desperate effort seemed in order. We launched into it.

We argued, cajoled and pleaded with Parbhu, trying to pin him down. With remarkable sweetness and restraint, he answered our questions in great detail, telling us nothing. Parbati observed the proceedings with a gentle, amused contempt.

An hour later they were on their way. 'To the next temple,' I said. 'To loot someone's field,' said Dalip.

Whatever it was he did, he managed to get her 200 kg of grass a day plus other food.

Only, we didn't know how.

(September 1997)

SOHAILA ABDULALI

Elsewhere

Something is wrong in Champawadi. The sun is shining on the little settlement on the hill, the champa tree still sits at the foot of the hill, a purple sunbird calls out his sharp little December mating call, but Cottonia and I stand on the road, befuddled, because Champawadi is empty.

Cottonia is my rambunctious, lovable and extremely silly Great Dane. He lives with my family in a tribal district in rural Maharashtra, and he and I often go for walks past Champawadi, a tiny Adivasi hamlet on a tiny hill, named after the champa tree which straddles the nearby curve in the Chillar river.

Usually I drag Cottonia past this point as fast as I can, because the mangy little dogs in Champawadi have a tendency to tumble out of their houses, along with dozens of children, as we go by, and they scream and shout and scare my cowardly dog. Cottonia is huge, but no one has ever accused him of being either sensible or courageous. The Champawadi dogs, while tiny, are feisty and alarming and Cotto is always happy to give them a wide berth. So where are they today, and what about the children?

Champawadi is a picture book village; from a distance it looks like the 'little Gaulish village' in Asterix comics. About ten roofs, of tile and thatch, huddled together on the crest of the little hillock, with a path leading down to the river. In the monsoon, it sits amidst an emerald landscape of waterfalls and tiger-lilies. The children are naked or in rags, and without exception beautiful. Usually when I walk by, plenty of them come and stand on the hill and giggle at me. Today there are no children, no dogs, no women swaying down to the river to beat their clothes into submission. Yeshwant Pingle, a local bigwig, roars up on his motorcycle out of a cornucopia of red dust, and pulls up when he sees me. '*Kaay re*, baby? Wandering again?'

'Yeshwant, where are all the Champawadi people? I don't see Leela or anyone.'

Yeshwant, who makes his living filling riverbed sand in his truck and selling it to builders, waves dismissively in the direction of the hill. 'They're gone. Nothing to fill their stomachs, so they left. They went off in some contractors' lorries, to find work.'

'But—all of them? What about the old people? And the children? And the animals?'

'Arre, what do they know? They couldn't fill their stomachs, and they went.' He explains that the whole village had gone into collective debt at Ganpati time, borrowing lots of money so they could have a huge drunken debauch, and also pay off the local moneylender with more borrowed money. The kind contractor had given them all they wanted and more, on the condition that he would come after Diwali and take them away to work off their debt. They had bonded themselves to him without hesitation, all of them.

Yeshwant spits contemptuously onto the road. 'Motherfuckers,' he says in Marathi. 'They don't want anything better. Arre, are they human even?'

I stare up at Champawadi, while Cottonia and Yeshwant warily eye each other. The eight odd houses there huddle silently. I think of all the people who have become familiar to me over the years— like Leela.

Leela and her husband Ram came to work for us about five

years ago, and it was an unmitigated disaster. My parents offered them a *pukka* place to stay, and in exchange for that and a good salary, Ram would work in the garden and Leela in the house, doing the cleaning etc. They arrived with two children, a boy and a girl with incongruously golden hair around their black shining faces. Ram started cutting grass and I started teaching Leela what was needed in the house. Leela had never been in a house before. In order to tell her she should dust a table, I had to first explain what a table was. She looked silently at me as I took her around the house, and the more I babbled on, the more intimidated I was by her silence and simply by her looks. She was one of the most beautiful women I've ever seen—the chiselled face of an ancient Egyptian statue, perfect carriage, perfect skin. By the time I got to the last room, I had to stop myself from throwing myself at her feet and apologizing for being all wrong, in my shorts and short hair. I gave her some buckets and *pochcha* cloths, and went out into the garden to recover.

Later, I went back in to see how things were going. Half the living room floor was spotless, the other half full of muck and dog hair, and lying in the middle was a bucket of grey water, with a cloth beside it. I went out—back to Leela's house. She was sitting in front of the door, in the shade of a gliricidia tree, in my grandmother's chair. With one hand she held a mirror; with the other, she combed her hair in slow, concentrated, sensuous strokes. Flowers lay near her, ready to go into her braid. I stared. 'Um—are you going to finish washing the floor?' 'No.' She continued combing. Defeated, I crept back into the house and waited for a few hours until she came in to pick up the bucket.

Things were a little better in the garden, as Ram was used to doing agricultural labour, but between the golden-haired children plucking all the flowers and the whole family squatting with their *lotas* in the middle of the garden every morning, we soon parted ways. However, I had seen Leela often over the years. She was often washing her clothes in the river when I walked by, and she was always friendly. The children were growing up as stunning as their mother. Ram took to drink and rapidly started to look old.

Champawadi without Leela seems all wrong. Champawadi without *noise* seems all wrong. In the wedding season, these few households create an amazing amount of noise. They hire a loudspeaker, bring in truckloads of revellers and barrels of mahua liquor, and as the night goes on, everyone gets smashed beyond redemption, grabs the microphone whenever he or she gets a chance, and bawls out songs, lectures, scoldings and philosophy to the rest of the valley. I remember one night old Mati, who was annoyed at my father for something or the other—they have a long tradition of fighting with each other and coming back for more—monopolized the mike for a twenty-minute drunken denunciation of my father and all his faults, screamed out into the night air for all to hear. My father rolled his eyes while the rest of us laughed until we cried. The next day Mati was back to work with a deathly hangover and her usual irresistible smile for my father. Did Mati go in a lorry with Leela and Ram?

'They're not human,' Yeshwant repeats, restarting his bike. 'They don't want anything better. I'm telling you, baby.'

I think of Leela sitting and combing her hair so fastidiously. Surely she wanted something better. Wherever she is, breaking rocks, mixing cement, I hope she has plenty of time to comb her hair. But may be her comb is in her abandoned hut, waiting for the lorry to bring her back as it surely will before the next monsoon.

I find out later that before she left in the lorry, she hastily married off both the golden-haired children, adolescents now. The boy went to work; the girl to her new village. Such are the logistics of abandonment; the bizarre conventions of migration. So many millions of people, everywhere, leaving their homes to go off in lorries, on camels, in boats, to try to fill their stomachs, to pay off some debt. And how do you decide what to leave, what to take? In Champawadi, they didn't have too many possessions to worry about. Their clothes went with them, and so did their chickens. Their buffalo and goats were distributed to Adivasi relatives in nearby villages. What to take, what to leave? Leave your daughters behind, take your hens with you. These are the rules of leaving in a lorry. Give away your gleaming pots, abandon your dogs.

I walk up the path to the cluster of huts. Brick, bamboo, mud and dung, depending on the wealth of the occupant. On the roofs, bits of plastic—the ubiquitious green, blue and pink plastic bags which festoon all India. Dried mango leaves hanging in door-ways. A small stable stands empty, with pieces of rope on the dung floor. A lone bullock cart wheel hangs from a spoke. Piles of saw-dust, an empty liquor bottle, a single ragged black plastic chappal lie in forlorn disarray in the middle of the sunny courtyard around which the houses are ranged. On one of the doors, Ajay Devgan smiles in toothy splendour from the latest movie-poster. There are pictures of the stars of *Jung, Trimurti, Rangeela,* stuck with care on the door but becoming frayed in the sunny December winds. The sun shines and the sunbird is still screeching in the trees, but there is a terrible sadness about this empty place. I look out, at the river, the mountains all around, at the pink and gold grass, a field of mung, an egret flying languorously toward a lone black buffalo on the other side of the green water. It is an incredible view, achingly beautiful, but beauty doesn't fill your stomach, so they are gone, Leela, Ram, all the others.

Everybody hates the Adivasis, it seems. I think of Mati with her world-embracing guffaw, laughing at my wit when I point to an airplane and say there are people inside that thing; Leela with copper pots on her head, climbing up from the river, another precious Indian image rooted in poverty and oppression like so many of the pictures we hold so dear; Ram and his friends fishing in the river all day rather than working. Why do they enrage us so?

Lazy, lazy, says Yeshwant, but aren't there days he would rather fish in the river than collect mud from its banks? They are liars and crooks, generous to the point of literally giving away whatever they have, possessive to a fault, seething with passion, quick to anger, quick to tears, quick to hide in the bottle which we have forced down their throats, distractable as children. Just like Yeshwant, just like me, in so many things, but neither Yeshwant nor I can laugh or dance like Mati.

Suddenly Cottonia's ears perk up as he stares at the half-open door of one of the huts. A moment later the silence is shattered by yelps and roars as three dogs I recognize come out from their shelter. Two males, and a stringy bitch who used to terrify Cotto in the old days. Now, he leaps into their midst leaving me standing in the clearing with a bloody palm where the leash was yanked out of my hand. 'Cottonia, NO!' I scream, with visions of him torn apart by these wild desperate dogs. But, true to form, Cotto ignores me completely and I watch as he chases the dogs round and round the clearing, gets in a few nips here and there, and finally, chases them out. When I go to the edge of the village, I can see the bitch running for her life, already half a kilometre away, tail between her legs, yelping in a loud terrified peal.

Cotto comes back and stands triumphant in the clearing, pedigreed ears lolling, well-fed mouth frothing with delight and excitement. I look at him and feel obscurely guilty. He doesn't understand anything, stupid dog. I have to get him out of here.

In the distance, the mongrels are still squealing and running. It feels like the end of India.

(January 1997)

SIDDHARTHA DEB

Going Home

The Brahmaputra Mail may have been one of the longest trains running through the country, but I had been through most of its territories. Bar one. In its east-west journey from Dimapur to Delhi, taking on board the increasing numbers of my generation choosing to exchange the close, violent intimacy of the North-East for the personal growth and anonymity of the metropolis, it mapped out my own shifts. The only place I never knew was the starting point, the closest I got to it being a yellow signboard on a vacant platform starting imperatively, 'Change here for Dimapur', as I wandered disconsolately at Lumding junction. Caught, at these moments, halfway between Guwahati and Silchar, family and friends, I never really considered changing tracks—Dimapur remained part of that territory whose position in my life is prenatal. Only now, having run myself dry in the cities for ten years, I wanted to go there, on the Brahmaputra Mail.

The portents, however, were not good. 'No one', a cousin from the North-East had said, 'but no one, goes to Dimapur on that train. Guwahati's as far as you get. Take a bus from there. Everyone does.' Then he paused, remembering hill courtesies, 'Come to Shillong, enjoy yourself for some time, meet—,' he mentioned a name that meant nothing to me, 'then, you can go to Dimapur.'

The train left on time, drawing out of Old Delhi station under darkening skies, the unusual April rain bringing my destination closer. Two men with pock-marked faces who looked like father and son sat face to face eating peanuts as I settled into my lower berth, squeezing my bag in among sacks and suitcases and cartons. There was a lot of stuff being transported here, but at least I had a window seat, an important compensation on a journey that promised little except to get me to a point where real travel, hopefully, would begin.

I had some faint notions of my terminus: Dimapur, the last of Assam's flatlands and now a part of Nagaland in one of those administrative sleights of hand. It appeared in my mind as a lost station, trying vainly to recreate the bustle of the plains with its nondescript squalor, trapped in a permanent transition between hills and plains. My fellow passengers said we were expected to arrive at Guwahati at 11 a.m. the day after. 'But they slow the train down just beyond Balatown in Bihar.' Why? 'It's Bihar,' someone said. 'No, because they don't pass trains at night through Kokrajhar.' No one spoke of Dimapur.

Allahabad at 4.30 a.m. was faint cries of tea and the glistening shell of empty platforms. The river looked small, especially when compared to my memories of what we were moving towards. The town appeared as a blackened decay of buildings hanging just beyond the edge of the tracks but as we began pulling out the streets looked straight and an old-world charm nestled the houses and courtyards in sleep, speaking of new beginnings.

This is the scene where the traveller arrives to the unknown future stretching out before him, hesitant and unwilling to sever himself from the instrument that has brought him there and is his last link with the self he has known so far. Naipaul sees this as a central trope, the enigma of arrival, though the picture he has in mind—always the islander—frames a ship berthed at a port and a solitary figure with its back to it, facing the unknown town that lies ahead.

But a ship is too exotic, even ancient for most of us. For a continental like me, the liminal point is always the station, the beginning of the story inevitably amid a cloud of smoke and the clatter of crockery at the station restaurant. And that is why, you understand, even this nondescript train, whose only remarkable feature was the absence of caterers and that it had been blasted by Bodo insurgents about a year ago, had the possibility of romance for me. But it was, even I acknowledged, a faint possibility. It was not even the longest train—that status was denied it—and what I remembered about the narrow-gauge track from my journeys on the other line from Lumding may have changed for good.

My mother's family had been in the railways for three generations—nothing grand, station-masters and controllers—and it was one of my grandfather's colleagues who had talked about the Lumding track when it was being pushed forward towards the Naga Hills. It was one of the last expansions by the British—fifty years after Independence the conversion to broad-gauge was still going on—and Mukherjee Dadu's eyes had lit up. Listening to him, it was easy to fall prey to the romance of the North-East Frontier Railways at a time when it had undisputedly been the frontier.

'Camps, snakes, malaria . . .,' he had said fondly, 'We even got a jungle allowance.' And even with my greenhorn memory I could recall the journey home from a college in Calcutta, intolerably slow after Lumding as the train shook its way through a series of tunnels, halting in the middle of nowhere as long green staves of bamboo were lashed to the sides, and then a fleeting glimpse of Jatinga. I could never be there in August, the month when flocks of birds committed mass suicide by dashing into the ground, but there were always the silent tribals on the platform, red deer carcasses spread out on elephant ear leaves before them. They never looked up at you, even the transaction was carried out with averted eyes, and as the train pulled out the scene was still there, a ritual wedding feast which had been briefly invaded by rude city-dwellers.

For human beings, it is always ironic and bewildering, this reverse migration and return journey. Ten years ago I was dying to get out, to leave behind small-town life with its tiny streets cast in a permanent afternoon trance. And now here I was on a slow train, transferring my quest back to the very place where it had germinated. It was not a wholly liberating feeling, there was far too much anxiety about what I would find; the world I was going back to was neither old and familiar nor completely new.

In the morning, as we sped through Mughalsarai, Buxar, Ara, a little of the bustle and anxiety of journeying I had filled the sleepless night with came aboard with the local passengers and their segmented journeys. On the upper berth, a man in a uniform and thug moustache slept on without worry. He had no cause to bother about the ticket collector. There were two family groups with us now. A fat man parked his wife and two children on us while he argued successfully with the collector. There was also an old man with a young daughter who had boarded the train at Ara. He slept with his head thrown back while the girl stared at the floor. Their presence was somehow a more effective reminder of the idea of the family than the other self-contained group, the very roughness in this picture—the distance between their years, the absence of the mother or any siblings, and the overwhelming silence that was characteristic of their presence—emphasizing the bonds and fragmentations of a household.

In the evening, the Damodar lay outside my window, a massive sandbank marked with the snakes and ladders of rivulets and small bridges. Country and city were juxtaposed together, a profusion of trucks and tractors frantically loading sand, dominating the scene, broken up only at the edges by a few fishermen swinging their nets and a solitary boat.

At Bhagalpur the great rush of passengers who had boarded at Mughalsarai descended, but a new crowd, fresher, more purposeful, flowed in. The train had been declared a local for now and would stop at every station up to Sahibganj. We were lucky. Someone had been murdered further ahead. 'All trains, including 352 Down', the speaker cackled, giving 352 Down an importance that was taken away as swiftly, 'are being stopped for now.'

The Brahmaputra Mail chugged on, approaching the point where there had been trouble. The local passengers got nervous at the possibility of a delay, of failing to make it home till late at night. For us, however, this was only the first of many possible disruptions and we could afford to be tolerant, take the long-term view. A spate of train robberies had taken place in Bihar—people killed, a woman abducted—and Chief Minister Laloo Prasad Yadav and Railway Minister Ram Vilas Paswan had traded passionate insults as only friends turned foes can. There had been stories of gangs armed with AK-47s whom the railway police were too ill-equipped to handle and of the Bihar Military Police being pressed into service. We had seen no signs of them though, only at night the mandatory railway police with clumsy .303 rifles and massive Eveready flashlights.

Outside Shivnarayanpur, the train stopped. People milled around on the tracks, caught between hope and despair, while the engine ticked over slowly by itself. The crew came back together, all of them at various stages of buttoning their trousers, and the crowd scurried back. After fifteen minutes we came into Pirpainti, the trouble spot, and the first glimpse was of uniforms and guns on the platform. It felt good, this sudden status, an armed guard placed solely for us, and one imagined a screaming mob barely held in check, and the mêlée that would descend upon the station after we passed.

There was an uneven boundary wall beyond which men in

lungis and unshaven faces stood before ragged tenements, watching. The train slowed down, the men clambered over the wall, the police raised their rifles and voices, they scattered, re-forming in a line behind the wall, and the train was through. 'Now', everyone smiled in a sudden show of unity, the unreserved passengers brightest of all, 'there'll be no problem.'

Among the hordes who had clambered on at Bhagalpur, there was a group of Vaishnavite devotees, two old Bengali couples and a young man. My fellow passengers, chastened so far in the presence of the mob that had swirled all over the compartment, turned belligerent with them, their hesitation as they nervously asked if they could sit making them easy targets.

They didn't need much room as they stood in the passageway, shrunken people with white sandalwood paste smeared on their foreheads and carrying little bundles, but they were out of sorts in the secular world they were passing through. They still functioned in family units, however, the couples hanging together while the young man went off to the door. One of the older men brought *puri-sabzi* for himself and his wife. The train began to pull out while he fumbled for his cash. The boy selling the food got hysterical and abusive. It was pathetic to see how they had no reply to the aggression everywhere—they had neither peace nor rage—and I understood for the first time in my life why people would surrender to an institution that made passivity a virtue. It was easy to see them going about their menial chores at their ashram, bullied by the guru's close confidantes and rewarded in the evening by being allowed to close their eyes and sway their heads as the devotional songs built up to a crescendo.

The *puri*-seller remained on the train. It did him no harm because he had a monopoly on the carriage. The other couple became his customers and the same drama was re-enacted. The vendor screamed at the woman, she nudged her husband and asked him to hurry, he snapped back. It was not a pleasant pic-

ture. I asked the man next to me, the one who had been object-
ing most vociferously, to let the women sit. But they were clearly
out of luck, for a little while later the third passenger got off the
upper berth and they had to make way.

After more than twenty-four hours, as the train sped through
its second and last night, the introductions began. We were an
odd group to have waited so long, but perhaps the length of the
journey made everyone defer the moment. A packet of long
bidis was being distributed by the younger of the pock-marked
pair. It was a good *bidi,* with a distinct bitter flavour, unlike the
mass circulation *bidis* of the cities. An important barrier had
been breached, and the man smiled. 'From Pune,' he explained—
the *bidis,* not him. He and his father were from Rajasthan, traders
who ran a business in Along. I had no idea where that was. 'West
Siang District.' That didn't help either, so I took out a map and
he showed me, the district headquarters in fact, with a population
below 5,000 according to the map. They would get off just before
Guwahati, he said, and take another train part of the way. A train
into Arunachal Pradesh? Yes, there was one part of the way, he
said, even though it was very crowded.

'Come with us,' he suggested, with both the trader's canniness
as well as traditional second-class friendliness, but then he frowned,
'There's a bus strike. Did you know?' I knew: it was an all-India
transport operator's strike but it was expected to terminate by the
time we reached. No one else looked worried.

There were the two other men who were travelling together,
a thin one who played cards with the loner next to me, and a fat
one who sat opposite me. This was unfortunate, since he slept and
smirked alternately—it was one of those naturally smug faces—
and whenever I looked up from something I was reading, I would
see him with either his mouth open or his lips pressed together in
a tight arc.

The nondescript man next to me turned out to be a sepoy—
that was the word he used—with the BSF. It was his first posting

in the North-East, he said, looking far too happy for me. I decided to scare him a little with horror stories of insurgents. Where
exactly in the North-East? Tura, Garo Hills, he replied. It was I
who was disappointed. There were no guerrillas there worth
getting scared of, just the occasional robbers. He was joining two
months late, he explained, and planned to go back home as
soon as he had registered. He had no intentions of remaining
for long in some god-forsaken place, it was only a job after all.
Were you in Kashmir, I asked? He nodded: 'Before the insur-
gency became big. By the time militants began running round
the place, I had been posted to Delhi.' I gave up. He was one of
those lucky ones.

The train moved slowly through the Farakka barrage, approaching Malda. The barrage had been the source of some
trouble between passengers and government. The West Bengal
government had decided to impose a toll on the barrage which
was added to the passenger fare on long-distance trains passing
through. For some odd reason, probably an administrative error,
the Kanchanjunga Express was made exempt while the Darjeeling Mail, which also started in Sealdah, had to pay the toll.
Sharp-eyed travellers (they had to be Bengalis) noticed and protested. The government had an explanation. The tax was only
applicable to sleeper-class passengers and, since by definition
that meant passengers using their berths to sleep, Darjeeling
Mail passengers had to pay up. Their train crossed Farakka at
night while Kanchanjunga went through at ten in the morning
when no one was, or should be, sleeping.

I had no idea whether I was paying the toll or not. It was
just nine, still more than twelve hours left for Guwahati and
after that probably another day to Dimapur, but the lights had
dimmed and heads and feet protruded from the berths. I walked
around, watching the space between the toilets filling up with
large bales wrapped in local red-checked towels called *gamchas*.
I asked them what was inside. 'More *gamchas*, Dada.' They were

being taken from Malda to Coochbehar in North Bengal, apparently much in demand there.

There are no insomniacs on a train, only early risers. Even in that deep, unearthly slumber that permeates the train, the heavy breathing, a bunk creaking, a sudden wail, there is a certain licence to be awake. Sitting up, one is greeted by others maintaining an undercurrent of activity, an old man with his knees drawn up, the pulsating glow of a *bidi* as someone sucks on it once more, a passenger gathering his bags for the approaching station and the murmur of voices, fading and rising, from the freetrippers at the door.

There was no appreciable increase in speed, even though we were on an electric line again from Malda. There was a gap from Mughalsarai to Malda when the train ran on diesel, four generators of 25,000 Volts each running in succession to provide the power needed for this greying monster, already short of breath after over a 1,000 miles of dust. From New Jalpaiguri, it was a single-track line, still in broad gauge, so that a train had to be halted at a platform to let another pass. Fifteen hundred litres of diesel in four hours, I mused, as a substitute for 25,000 Volts from the power lines above, wondering idly whether I should work out the costs.

'Fifteen, you must be joking, Dada, I don't have time to waste.' I thought I was dreaming but it was a real voice at my ear, announcing the arrival of the morning in the incessant patter of the North Bengal hawkers. Like old-time pedlars they prowled the carriage, waking everyone but the most stubborn, with their anguished 'last prices' and new-age products. There was an energy about them not usually associated with the indolent east. They all looked similar, men caught between youth and middle age—one large bag, binoculars and vividly coloured pens hanging from the neck, a dozen watches, red cameras, black cassette recorders and torches in their hands—casually manoeuvring between carriages with no vestibule and reappearing suddenly to knock the price down once more, all the while managing to maintain an air of indifference and even contempt.

My trader friend was up, deeply interested in the wares, though not in the dry cell and ICB gizmos on display. He scrupulously examined, haggled and bought a dozen bras in six different colours for sixteen rupees each. The vendor soon had competition; his friends had been watching and they had smelt the blood of a professional buyer.

They had been around in the North Bengal sector for as far as I could remember and could be terribly aggressive with newcomers, especially with people who quoted what they thought was an unrealistically low price for something they didn't want. I remember one man being forced to buy a bicycle pump even though at the end he protested tearfully that he didn't have a bicycle to use it on.

They made one run a day, from New Jalpaiguri to New Coochbehar—like the hawkers the 'New' too had been around a long time—making a profit of around Rs 200 a day. If the figure they told me was on the lower side, as it must have been, they made decent money. 'One run a day is enough. Imagine making more than a couple of journeys on these trains,' a character in a dashing yellow shirt and porcupine hair told me, conveying an air of disinterested charity before he rushed off towards the next compartment.

There was more commotion around the Rajasthani trader now. The bra seller had come back. Two plastic packets were taken out, examined with great interest and bargained down from Rs 350 each to Rs 125. It was a long process, continuing up to the point the train left Coochbehar (Old), when the hawker suddenly thrust the packets at the trader through the window, ran along counting the cash, and disappeared suddenly as the platform gave way to the sight of yellow fields.

The whole process had been watched very closely by everyone in the compartment. 'What are those?' the sepoy finally asked.

'Like nighties, from neck to ankle. The hill girls love it,' he replied with a genial, proprietorial smile that no doubt had as much to do with the hill girls who wore these as with the killing he had made. I took a closer look at the package and read, 'Body stocking open at the crotch.'

North Bengal had become Assam without any noticeable change in landscape. Only the Assam bungalow, a variation of the Essex Cottage, with corrugated sloping roofs, raised floor and bamboo-and-plaster walls spoke of new lands.

(The walls of one of our rooms had broken off, exposing its bamboo skeleton. Lying on my side, bored by the wet patches which no longer resembled maps or faces, I began to scrabble around, hoping, not to find a secret passage but to break on through to the other side, until my father caught me at it.)

There was also an increase in the frequency of rivers, and I braced myself for the sight of the Brahmaputra. We passed through Kokrajhar in daylight, as empty and unpromising in the swift eastern sun as at midnight. Beyond the station was the blast site. There were bent, twisted carriages lying below the embankment, carving out their own burial pits in the soft grass like slaughtered elephants. The fat-thin pair, railwaymen or an inspection tour, spoke up. The target, the fat one said, was two army bogies carrying troops from a regiment that had captured Bodo insurgents. 'Revenge,' he said with gloomy satisfaction. He was not smirking now. They got most of the train, the air-conditioned carriages were on the other side. 'There,' he pointed at a clump of grass that rose like an island in a green sea: 'That's from where they used the remote.' How did they know? He was on solid ground now, he must have really been there in the new year, watching with his friends as the combat uniforms and paramedics and reporters swarmed among the dying and the dead. 'They used sniffer dogs.' RDX, I asked. Yes.

Running an hour late, the train grew wings, racing ahead

of its shadow and the debris of the ultimate bad trip. There had been a mandatory police check of baggage just after Kokrajhar, and almost as soon as it was over, as if at a signal, bundles were dragged out, slippers and *lungis* put away and everyone sat up in shoes and socks with a perceptible 'let's get to work' mood. The traders were worried. They would get off at Kamrup, just before Guwahati, but if they had a problem with their next train, they would be spending money in going to Guwahati again for a bus.

They disappeared in a sudden flurry of activity, a final cluster of *bidis* pressed into my hand, blurs on the platform dwarfed by their goods, like fading characters from a picaresque waiting to be resurrected someday when the scene moves to a grocer's store at Along, West Siang district.

The bridge appeared first, and then the river, as the train thundered through and coins flew out like metal sparks from the second-class carriages, striking the rafters. There was an exultant yell from the thin railwayman, 'You hit the tracks, I told you—always in a parabola.' We had arrived in another country.

I sat by myself in an empty compartment by a nearly empty platform as women washed themselves around a tap, placing their screaming children on the flat basin around the raised water-spouts. Everyone had departed, and without the hum of the 25,000-Volt genie I sat like Aladdin without a lamp, the magic of a myriad voices and bodies gone. I went out and asked two uninterested vendors about when the train left for Dimapur. The suggestion was dismissed outright by the first man. The other one showed a little more grace. 'It leaves at 11.30, at night, catch B.G. Express from platform one to Lumding instead.' It was 1.30 p.m. No one knew about Dimapur, there were no cigarette shops on this platform or the next and my patience was beginning to run down. I left my luggage chained to the window and went to platform one, to the non-veg refreshment room where years ago a sweet-tempered old man had asked me to relax and have my chicken and rice, assuring me he would let me know well in advance about the train.

Food, I was told, would take time. How much time? Lots of time. The station-master's room was empty. I went back to the train. A police officer stopped me now. He was polite and shook his head gently, repeating that I had to take the B.G. Express, which was leaving now, if I wanted to proceed further. But how far? Up to Lumding, he said, beyond that the track was being converted to B.G., broad gauge. I unpacked my luggage, reluctant to make any decision, feeling defeated at having to adjust my plans even before the journey had really begun.

The B.G. Express was packed, there was no place to keep my bags while I tried—bags swinging from my shoulder, buffeted constantly by the crush of passengers—to explain to an incoherent ticket collector that I wanted a reserved berth. He didn't understand what I was saying. I got off the train in desperation as it began to leave, raising vexed shouts from those trying to board at the last minute.

The Deputy Station Manager was at his office. He confirmed that the Brahmaputra Mail terminated here. Why do you issue tickets all the way to Dimapur, I asked angrily. 'In Delhi,' he shrugged, they were both too far away to bother him. I collected my refund of thirty-eight rupees after the usual confusion of counters, and crossed the overbridge to the bus stand. There was a mob there, howling and shrieking with rage, women standing next to luggage and babies, men flooding the counters. There was a 100-hour 'chakka jam', strike, throughout the North-East and none of the private services was running. There were notices stating that government buses to Dimapur were full up to the next day and at the toilet, men scurried around in striped underwear holding mugs.

I watched like a complete stranger, trying to stave off the sense of hopelessness. I didn't want to spend a night in Guwahati. The alien mass slowly began to delineate itself: well-dressed Khasis carrying huge bags stuffed with loot from city department stores, surly army *jawaans* in twos and threes, Bengalis and North Indians—the most shabby dressers of all, accompanied by resentful families—all going somewhere, holding a password that seemingly circumvented the strike and the full buses and delay.

The Shillong counter was empty, and the fare two rupees more than what the railways had disgorged. When does the bus leave? Right now, hurry man, hurry, the man said, looking anything but frantic. The Assamese words began to come back slowly, haltingly, as like a fastidious tourist I asked him a string of questions. He answered patiently, yes it was a luxury bus and there was a window seat available and it was the last bus for the day to Shillong.

I decided to visit hometown.

(March 1998)

KAI FRIESE

Local Geography

At the entrance to my neighbourhood there is a large municipal map with the reassuring legend 'you are here'. Well, I presume it says something to that effect, but I can't say for sure because the alphabets of local geography, all the blocks from A to N have been entirely obscured by other inscriptions, peeling layers of posters for *Her Body* and other morning glories at nearby Eros cinema, and some offers of 'Weight Loose' at Slimline Health Club. If I were better-read I might delight in the *bricolage* of this defacement. In fact I feel territorial about Jangpura Extension and wish I could read the map. But lately, much of what I have been reading instead tells me my fondness for my neighbourhood is a strange perversion: 'topophilia',[1] or worse, a symptom of 'the phallocentric geographical gaze'.[2]

[1] The term was coined by the self-confessed topophile Y.F. Tuan, who describes my symptoms perfectly: 'fleeting visual pleasure; the sensual delight of physical contact; the fondness for place because it is familiar, because it is home and incarnates the past, because it provokes pride of ownership or creation: joy in things because of animal health and vitality'. Cited (disapprovingly) in *Feminism and Geography, The Limits of Geographical Knowledge* by Gillian Rose. p. 49.

[2] Gillian Rose, p. 101.

In the peculiar world of post-modern theory any attachment to place carries such stigma. It is hopelessly modern, which is to say, out of date. Needless to say, these texts give short shrift to the Nation, which as every literate person knows is a fiction, and of course an 'imagined community'.[3] There are at least two books that have planted this realization firmly on our shores: *Imagining India* and *India Imagined*.[4] Clearly, an insight that doesn't require much imagination.

Actually, it seems fairly obvious to me that the nation is an abstraction, that we usually experience rhetorically, and increasingly as a spectacle on our electronic hearths. India, I know only too well, is a magazine, several T.V. show, and countless songs. One particular song that rams home the point with unintentional vigour is the channel V-fuelled hit *I am an Indian* by the duo Noble Savages. 'I am an Indian, from Bombay city, I am an Indian so you better follow me', they growl to a ragga beat. Which is inane enough, but the video channel also broadcasts a short interview with the singers, who we learn are in fact from a small town in Germany. Their strongest memories of India are genetic. 'I tink its important for everyone to identify viz hiss country,' says the boy singer in his teutonically inflected *faux*-Jamaican brogue, and without a shred of irony.

So, yes, when it comes to the nation, I'm an imaginary Indian and not a noble savage. Yet somehow, the neighbourhood is a different matter. In my c'lony, I'm a native ... and a phallocentric topophile to boot. Jangpura Extension is for me the most concrete of territories. I traverse it daily on foot, leaving from the east and returning from the west (for complex but not cosmological reasons). I know its boundaries, which like any 'real' frontier are

---

[3]The thing to do, Iain Chambers suggests, is 'to pass from faith in an imagined "community" to the recognition of complex identities forged in discontinuous, heterogenous histories . . . to pass into a contingent world.' *Migrancy, Culture, Identity,* p. 102.

[4]If the titles are anything to go by, I haven't read them.

zones of nuisance, transition and danger. To the east there is Mathura road, where I must negotiate with the autowalas; to the south there is the railway *phatak* and its cranked barriers (just like a border crossing) that separate us from Lajpat Nagar; to the west, the murderous traffic of Josip Broz Tito Marg (or alternately an underpass where on dark nights you must run the gauntlet of hulking and sometimes elegant *hijras* who sell sex in the shadow of the Defence Colony flyover). To the north there is a sprawling *nala*, a former stream on whose further shore is a *kabristan*, a burning ghat and that whole stretch of what was once necropolitan Delhi, littered with the tombs of empires from the Sayyads to the Mughals. But never mind the thanatos, because returning to the heart of Jangpura we find Eros and its undoubtedly phallocentric delights. Turn right, turn left and left again, and I'm home.

That's my most basic map of Jangpura. It's crude, but it gives me a satisfying sense of orientation and centredness. It also means of course that I can't be truly PoMo. Why? Well, as Gayatri Chakravorty Spivak would tell you, 'it is this longing for a center, an authorising pressure, that spawns hierarchized oppositions.'[5] It's true. She's right. It does. Because my delight in my concrete locality inducts me into an understanding of the hierarchy of places I inhabit from the body, which is too intimate to routinely regard as a place, to the world, which is too expansive. It is in my neighbourhood that I can ground the cartographic metaphors that bridge the space between these places.

This is, I think, nothing unusual. Even Ed Said said as much in the preambulatory chapters of *Orientalism,* where he acknowledges the universal impulse of what he calls 'imaginative geography'. Referring to Gaston Bachelard's 'poetics of space' he writes: 'Space acquires emotional and even rational sense by a kind of poetic process, whereby the vacant or anonymous reaches

[5]Cited (reverently) by Iain Chambers, p. 71.

of distance are converted into meaning for us here'.[6] Yet the over-whelming intent of much modern, er, I mean contemporary, thought (including Said's) about geographical identity is a polemic against local sentiment. The ideal post–modern neighbour is a strange creature who cannot share the pleasure of location because his mind is elsewhere. The 'exile', the 'nomad' and the 'schizo' are the model citizens who crop up repeatedly in this literature. They are 'deterritorialized' and 'de-centred' individuals, and as far as I can tell they have no bearing on reality.[7]

But ho hum! Let's return to the natives of Jangpura Extension. Many of them are exiles, others are nomads of sorts, and at least a few are, I suspect, schizos. Yet most of them seem quite at home and well centred in their own cartographies.

Exilic Jangpura was first revealed to me by Mr Mohindra in E–27. Uncle Mohindra died last year and crossed the water to the *shamshan* ghat. But he remains the quintessential figure of a neighbour. He was already in his eighties when I got to know him, his orbit confined to the locality, but our paths usually crossed at least twice a day and he could enforce the ritual of a neighbourly chat with a reproachful glance as I passed the gate of Mohindra Niwas. I'm glad he did. Mr Mohindra remembered the days when the entire colony was a horizontal neighbourhood of single-storeyed homes *like* his own. He told me that blocks D and E had originally been allotted exclusively to refugees from Model Town, in Lahore, and he would reminisce about the spacious beauty of this lost neighbourhood. But one day we had a house guest from

---

[6] *Orientalism,* pp. 54–55. I haven't read Bachelard either. In Said's account at least, Bachelard's poetics of space are grounded not in the neighbourhood but in the home, which 'acquires a sense of intimacy, secrecy, security, real or imagined, because of the experiences that seem appropriate for it.' Sounds like topophilia to me.

[7] The exile is a particular favourite of Said's, the Schizo and the Nomad are the heroes of parts 1 and 2 respectively of Deleuze and Guattari's *Anti-Oedipus.* You can meet them all in Chambers' *Migrancy, Culture, Identity* as well.

Pakistan, from Model Town in fact, and he told me that the place was littered with modern monstrosities like our own *dholpur*-clad apartment block. Nothing remarkable, I suppose, but I liked the image of a map of a corner of Lahore being superimposed on Delhi's landscape and then erasing itself in similar ways in both places. I imagine that Jangpura's original template is similarly peopled with exiles-turned-stolid house owners, circuiting the municipal parks with their Pomeranian satellites at dusk.

Jangpura is of course a bourgeois neighbourhood. But that obvious term conceals as many geographies as it reveals. There are the territories of the Jamadarans, for example, purchased by auction from a contractor Mafia when the neighbourhood was being built half a century ago. Many of these enterprising crones still stalk the streets and hector their sub-contractees, the Bangladeshi rag-pickers along the shadowy network of service lanes. Then there are the residual Gujjars of Bhogal—the village that Jangpura swallowed—who manage to nourish their cattle in the *nalas* of the colony. Here along these grassy and acacia-lined embankments one can see strangely linear vistas of a vanished pastoral landscape which bring to life that old chestnut of New Delhiite conversation: 'I can remember when all this was kikar forest.'

One of the grandest houses in Jangpura belongs to the Lingtsangs, who are rumoured to be of the royal family of Kham in Northern Tibet. And Khampas are famously fierce itinerant pastoralists and brigands. But like nomads everywhere the Khampas do not roam around aimlessly. They have a strong sense of local geography, as does the growing tribe of Tibetans, who have been expanding their holdings in the neighbourhood around the original focus of the Lingtsangs' mansion, acquiring four new properties on our street in the past two years.

More straightforwardly nomadic are the shifting populations of Kashmiris and Afghans, who have a long tradition of wintering in Jangpura, driving up rents as they come, depressing the market, and the landlords, as they go. Lately the troubles in their summer pastures have made them a more constant feature, and a permanent anxious presence in the local STD booths. Some of the more strapping Afghans are amputees, a disturbing embodiment of their fractured homeland. But they seem at peace in the neighbourhood.

Clearly, Jangpura has many maps. Perhaps as many as it has inhabitants. This may seem perilously close to the dreaded postmodern vision of a geography whose centre doesn't hold. In fact, the feminist geographer Gillian Rose has a nice term for this perspective which certainly fits Jangpura too: 'plurilocality'. But I don't think this is a uniquely contemporary condition. Places are always weighted with multiple associations of the people who frequent them. In India certainly, this principle is often systematically applied in the superimpositions of sacred geography on the landscape, a system that also involves geographical transpositions, so that for example Kashi can be found in several locations, and many places are symbolically represented within the sacred circuit of Kashi.[8]

But this sort of complex geographical cosmology also requires an overarching grand plan within which plurilocality can be situated. I haven't actually seen one for Jangpura yet. Perhaps it's concealed beneath the posters on that municipal board. Probably not, but I do know what I'd like to find there: an Egocentric map.[9] This expressive name describes a distinctly pre-modern, and fortunately, oriental, cartographic technique, also known as Azimuthal Equidistant Projection. It was developed by the Arab mathematician Al-biruni about a thousand years ago. In an Egocentric map one's own location is represented as a point surrounded by the rest of the world. Distances from any point on the globe to the centre are accurately represented to scale but the map also has its own peculiar distortions. The antipode of your

[8]All right, I read Eck.

[9]A lovely name given to a lovely map in a lovely book: *Poetry of the Universe, a Mathematical Exploration of the Cosmos.* By Robert Osserman.

location, i.e., the point half-way round the earth from you, becomes the outer perimeter of the map. On my Egocentric map Jangpura would be surrounded by a circle representing a point off the coast of Chile. Such a map has many virtues. It is useful; its distortions are obvious; it acknowledges other people's maps, since every location demands its own Egocentric projection. And of course it gives Jangpura a pleasant maritime horizon.

The Egocentric map is for me an almost archetypal idea. But it has a necessary antipode of its own which also has a somewhat archetypal appeal. I found such a map described in a book by the psychoanalyst Anthony Storr: 'A patient of mine used to represent himself by drawing a circle. He had the fantasy of the circle expanding until it included the whole world, so that he and the whole world would finally be indistinguishable. He was a schizophrenic who was quite incompetent to deal with the world in fact.'

Between these two imaginative geographies I know I prefer the Egocentric map. The featureless Schizophrenic map, devoid of fixed points of reference, is, I fear, closer to the post-modern ideal. And it may well be a true map. A recent book by a French ethnologist Marc Augé[10] paints a disturbing but convincing picture of an expanding featureless world of 'non-places'. Augé suggests that at least in what he calls the 'advanced west' people spend a growing portion of their lives in the anonymity of transit or in anonymous replicable sites ranging from cash-point counters to Disney worlds. It is a world in which people are not spatially bound, and it is characterized by what he describes as a three-fold excess: an excess of space (linked to increasing mobility), of time (in the flood of 'events' that assail the individual) and an excess of references,[11] by which (crudely) he means that people must pay attention to signs rather than their environment. Supermodernity he calls it.

[10] *Non-Places, Introduction to an anthropology of supermodernity.*
[11] Like this.

I'd like to say *'bonne chance* Marc! Your world, not mine.' Here in Jangpura we are spatially bound, nothing much happens, and no one pays attention to signs.[12] But while Augé's vision is apparently descriptive, it is also more insidiously prescriptive. Hypermodernity is increasingly a global phenomenon, he argues: this is the fate of the world.[13] Like the schizophrenic's fantasy, the post-modern or supermodern imagination sees itself expanding to include the whole world.

Meanwhile, I continue to delight in the experience of my particular, local geography. In Jangpura.

(*Originally appeared in* Femina, *then in the* India Magazine *August 1997)*

[12]Sometimes at great personal risk: I once saw a man urinating off the top of a pedestrian overbridge which crosses the tracks from Jangpura to Lajpat Nagar. He was staring at a plaque with a red skull and crossbones, which promised him something like ten million volts, as his stream passed neatly between the high tension wires of the Delhi Circular railroad.

[13]'For we live in a world that we have not yet learned to look at. We have to relearn to think about space.' Augé pp. 35–36.

BISHAKHA DATTA

Death of a Tourist

In the forty-six years that he lived, Raymond Kelly* led an everyday sort of life. He passed his exams, albeit with distinction, he got a job, he married. Not twice, nor thrice nor a remarkable four times. Just once. But his death in Goa—violent, before its time, throat slashed red in an alien land—elevated him to an enigma, a riddle worth untangling, a mystery yet to be solved. Why would anyone want to kill Raymond Kelly?

Goa is the kind of place where tourism, after going up, up, up, has now slid over the top, so much so that a section of irate Goans has set up an army to protect itself from the swelling ranks of the Sunworshipping Lungifunghis. Yes, literally an army (even thought it doesn't believe in guns), the Goenkaranchi Fauj. Its finest hour dawned when it pelted a chartered planeload of arriving Germans with fresh cakes of cowdung. 'Cheers! Let's toast the new arrivals! Mud in your eye! Cheers! Cowdung on your collar! *Phachaak!* Welcome to Goa!'

Kelly may have been a sunworshipper, but he was not part of the charter crowd. Neither was he a Lungifunghi. He was a loner.

*Some of the names have been changed.

A Britisher working as teacher in Saudi Arabia, he had been to Goa several times before, usually by himself. In 1990, he spent a couple of weeks in the quieter, southern beaches of Goa around Colva, visiting the family of his colleague, the extravagantly named Brazinho Pascual D'Souza. 'His closeness (to D'Souza) is evident from the fact that certain photographs of the deceased along with the applicant's family were seized by local police,' a CBI report would later note, as if carrying photographs were a crime.

The following year, in 1991, Kelly came back to Goa, again alone, around the time of Diwali. He checked into the Nova Goa, a small hotel in Panjim, used more by businessmen than by tourists. Three days after he had checked into room 203, neighbours complained of a foul smell from that room. The door, which was locked from the inside, was broken down. Kelly was discovered lying on his bed in a pool of dried blood, his hands and legs tied behind his back, his throat slit and gaping. His travellers' cheques, passport and camera were missing. A broken *nanchaku,* found lying on the floor, was the only immediate clue. A post-mortem showed a large quantity of opium alkaloids in what was left of Kelly's bloodstream.

Was it a robbery gone wrong? A drug murder? A crime of passion? Or revenge? Why would anyone want to kill Raymond Kelly, not just kill him—but slit his throat so viciously that his head was almost severed from his torso? Why would anyone want to kill him so badly that they would first strangle him with a *nanchaku,* giving up only when it snapped and broke the tension on his throat? Why would anyone want to spill so much blood, enough to saturate the entire double mattress?

Nobody knows. Even today, five years later, nobody, not the Goa police, not the CBI which was called in to replace them, nobody is sure of what happened in room 203.

Except Paul Kelly. Back home in London, Paul, himself a bobby, swears on his dead brother's grave that he will avenge his death—lawfully. And he succeeds to some extent, both in getting the British press to cover the case and in getting the British Foreign Office to exert enough pressure to have the case transferred from the Goa police to the CBI, which is assumed to be a better detective.

Paul is convinced that his brother was the victim of a robbery that went awry, resulting in his murder. He comes down to Goa on his own. CBI investigations have already come up with two tenuous, but pivotal clues that point to the involvement of hotel employees: hotel room boy Henry Serrao's karate-crazy brother, Jerry Serrao, is a possible link with the *nanchaku;* a blood-stained shirt and Nova Goa bedsheet are found in the locker of another roomboy, Prakash Naik. Naik is significant for another reason: he is the room boy who took breakfast up to Kelly's room the morning after he checked in. He brought the breakfast back, claiming no one had opened the door. But if Kelly was already dead, who ordered breakfast from room 203 that morning?

By now Paul is completely convinced that the Serraos—Jerry and Henry—are his brother's killers. He feels they had planned to drug and rob Raymond; when the drug wore off midway through the robbery, they panicked and killed him to escape identification. He sees the breakfast order as a red herring, meant to foster the illusion that Kelly was alive. Confronted with a pile of evidence and witnesses who testify against him, Jerry Serrao breaks down and confesses. He admits to being part of a gang of four that had killed Kelly. The other three, he says, are well-known Goa gangsters; Henry was the outside guy who gave them the lead-in to Kelly. Henry and Jerry Serrao are arrested by the CBI. A few months later, they are set free.

Three years after the blood has dried on Raymond Kelly's corpse, I sit at police headquarters in Panjim, trying to wet my fingers in it. I have been hired by a London-based television company to research the case for a forthcoming documentary. Inspector Umesh Gaonkar, who originally investigated the case, sits opposite me. Gaonkar is officially on paternity leave, 'but they keep calling me in every day for one thing or another.'

Like everybody else in Goa, Gaonkar remembers the case vividly despite the passage of time.

'I was following four angles on the case,' he says. 'Homosexuality. Drugs. Spying. Robbery. But there was not enough evidence to pick one.'

But I thought it was a robbery attempt, and the Serrao brothers were involved, I feebly say.

'No, no, definitely not,' he says dismissively, as if it were out of the question.

'But what about the *nanchaku*?' I ask. 'Doesn't that implicate Jerry Serrao?'

'I have a *nanchaku* at home,' says Gaonkar. 'Does that mean I was involved?'

My sand castle is rapidly crumbling and I must try to save it.

'But the CBI arrested the Serraos,' I assert. Authority is always a last resort for the desperate.

Gaonkar smiles, a quiet, conspiratorial smile with a hint of triumph. 'You know how the CBI works,' he says. The interview is over.

Gaonkar's solid presence gives way to the dynamo hum of Anthony Fernandes, a crime reporter with the *Goa Post*. Fernandes, twenty-eight, is every bit as brash as the paper he works for and he is convinced the murder was related to drugs.

'If you examine Kelly's itinerary, you'll see he was here on a drug mission,' he explains. 'Delhi–Benares–Delhi–Bombay–Goa. These are all drug points.'

These are all standard tourist spots too, I point out. I may not be Sherlock Holmes, but I haven't nursed my neurons for twenty-nine years for nothing.

Fernandes can account for this. 'He could not have been

here as a tourist,' he says. 'He was only to stay for two days. Why would a tourist stay in Panjim? And he never stepped out of his hotel to go anywhere. He must have been here to meet someone.'

'Like who?'

'Like Babuni.'

Babuni, I learn, is a well-known gangster and hitman with alleged links to the Goa Protectors, the Goan version of the Shiv Sena. Fernandes insists that Kelly was seen strolling in Panjim with a Babuni look-alike. And Babuni bought a flat soon after the murder, which was constructed with money from the murder. Or so Fernandes believes.

I don't know what to make of this theory. On the one hand, Fernandes obviously takes his crime reporting seriously. Why else would he visit every film-processing store in Panjim to track down the whereabouts of an empty roll of Konica film that was found in Kelly's trash can? On the other hand, Fernandes was badly beaten up by the Goa Protectors a few years ago (he needed eighteen stitches) and bears a deep grudge against them. His insistence that Babuni is the killer: is it based on a deep understanding of crime developed over the years? Or does he have his own axe to grind?

The British side, meanwhile, is trying to grind its own inexplicable axe; I am asked to contact Murshid Zaman, a youth who had a chat with Raymond Kelly on a train from Benares to Delhi— three years ago! He lives in a village near Patna called Mahendru, but the British TV crew is optimistic about tracing him. 'If his memory needs jogging, it was coach 1964, compartment A, lower berth,' Mark, the assistant producer, faxes me. I dutifully drop Zaman a postcard, knowing full well no reply will arrive.

Mark and I have set up our own Transcontinental Detective Hotline by now. Like two amateur sleuths, we are both hooked— not just on the story, but on what actually happened to Kelly.

Every other day, we spend much of his company's fortunes comparing notes long-distance, London-Goa. I am beginning to get quite addicted to these sessions.

'So what's the local verdict?' Mark asks, during one session.

'Well no one in Goa thinks its the Serraos,' I reply. 'They feel it's Babuni, some local gangster.'

'Aah, a goomba,' says Mark, knowledgeably.

'Goomba?' I ask, wondering if I have heard right.

'Yes goomba, you know, Indian thug.'

'Aah, yes, goomba,' I ad-lib rapidly. He means *goonda,* of course.

I love the way Westerners inevitably chew up Indian words and ideas and spit them out as global sound bites. Charlie Pye-Smith, a British travel writer, in his book *Travels in Nepal* refers to 'Shiva, the long-haired Hindu goddess'. I have now connected these two germs of malapropism into my own compendium of quintessential British follies: 'Miss Murgatroyd has set her goombas onto Shiva, the long-haired Hindu goddess.'

I have been to Goa several times without any particular fear that the palm tree will rise up and strangle me. But goombas, particularly when connected with drugs, are a different kettle of fish. Mopping up a hearty breakfast of muesli, fruits, garlic cheese, pancakes, yoghurt and scrambled eggs at the Milky Way, I set out on the Great Goomba Hunt. My first stop is Dona Paula, where I am scheduled to meet Rajan Narayan, editor of the newspaper *O Heraldo,* and a king maker of sorts.

The lights have gone out in Narayan's house when I arrive. Narayan sits bare-chested in a cane chair, a towel wrapped around his hips, writing what he calls an 'idiotorial'. He holds his pen awkwardly, as if it is a foreign instrument. Perhaps he is in pain; he is recovering from two severe attacks on him, also by the Goa Protectors, which have left him partly blind and paralysed from the waist down. An armed commando accompanies him when he goes out; a policeman keeps guard outside his house round the clock. The cop is not in his chair when we get there;

his uniform lies there instead. 'He has left it there symbolically,' laughs Narayan.

Narayan completely pooh-poohs the Serrao/robbery theory; he too is convinced this was a drug killing. According to him, Kelly was a drug dealer who was visited by known drug dealers in his room. The German drug mafia hired Babuni to kill him, since he was cutting into their drug network. He insists the killing was deliberately brutal to set an example for other newcomers and claims that one million pounds was discovered in Kelly's room, something I have never heard before. And he is equally insistent that the Goa Police hushed up the case since Babuni enjoys the patronage of MLA Zuwarkar, and Zuwarkar's brother-in-law was in the police at that time.

Back at the police station, Inspector Bosco George *giggles* when I ask him if Babuni killed Kelly; his belief is that Babuni is too noticeable to commit such a crime. 'Every time Babuni makes a public appearance in Panjim, people say "There's Babuni . . . there's Babuni." From George's description, Babuni emerges as a Gulliver in a land of pygmies—seven feet tall and almost as wide. Jerry Serrao, in his confession, had sketched how the gang of four, including Babuni, scaled the hotel walls and inched along the parapet to reach Kelly's room in the dead of night. 'Jerry can do that sort of stuff,' giggles George. 'But Babuni is too big, he cannot climb parapets and all. He has to go through the normal channels . . . doors and all.'

I look sceptical. George tries a different tack. 'Find Babuni,' he says. 'See for yourself.'

'Where will I find him?' I ask. I don't really expect an answer.

'Go ask MLA Zuwarkar,' says George. 'But don't tell him I told you to go to him.'

This is getting more and more bizarre—a policeman is telling me to go to a Congress politician to locate a seven-foot goomba.

'And what will I tell Zuwarkar?' I inquire, in my most sarcastic manner. 'That I'm looking for a suspected killer, and you may be sheltering him?'

George is unperturbed. 'Just tell Zuwarkar you've heard Babuni is a party worker,' he says, in a cheery Bertie Wooster-like manner.

Election fever is raging in Goa as I reach MLA Zuwarkar's house in Taleigaon, on the outskirts of Panjim. The Assembly elections are just a month away, television crews from all around the world are frantically interviewing Churchill Alemao, Pratapsinh Rane, Wilfred 'Willy' D'Souza, and other ministerial hopefuls. A frisson of excitement runs through a Zuwarkar household as I announce that I represent a TV crew from London. Zuwarkar hurries out, dressed in knickers and banian, beaming widely. He believes I have come to cover the elections. He pumps my hand vigorously, looking deep into my eyes. A power handshake. A chilled Coke is simultaneously thrust into my other hand.

'I'm trying to find a party worker called Babuni,' I say, after introducing myself. The hand is rapidly withdrawn; Zuwarkar moves two steps back and starts to stutter. 'Babuni?' he says. 'Who is he?' 'He's your party worker,' I say, looking confused. 'I was told he would be with you.' Zuwarkar decides it is time to get rid of me, Coke and all. 'No, no, I don't know any Babuni,' he mutters rapidly. 'He hangs out in Santa Cruz or somewhere.' If you don't know Babuni, how do you know where he hangs out, I want to ask. Instead I slurp down my Coke and leave before he throws me out.

A broken *nanchaku*. A missing camera. An Englishman in Goa. Somewhere between these disparate items lies the truth. Different pieces of the puzzle point in wildly differing directions. The *nanchaku* points to the brothers Serrao. The missing camera points to robbery. The presence of opium alkaloids in Kelly's body points to drugs. And Kelly's diary, which his brother mysteriously burnt—

even though, as a cop, he realizes the importance of preserving all evidence? What does one make of that? The diary, with occasional descriptions of 'men kissing one another' and 'penises swinging high and low', opens the door on Kelly's homosexual leanings. But what does that have to do with murder, other than the fact that a nation of sexual hypocrites will always equate homosexuality with dark, devious impulses? And what does one make of the fact that Kelly worked at British Aerospace in Saudi Arabia and came to India every year? Is that a material fact that points in the direction of spying? Or is that completely incidental, as beside the point as the information that he was one of nine children born to an Irish family which migrated to Britain?

Add to this a growing east-west divide. The British TV crew is completely convinced it was the Serraos; in Goa everyone believes it was Babuni. London insists it's a robbery; Goa insists it's drugs. I am stuck in the middle of this transcontinental chorus. I share my confusion with Mark, who explains that the programme will objectively accommodate all points of view. But I know that when push comes to shove, the programme will stand by a British viewpoint: a Londoner out to secure justice for his English brother innocently murdered in savage India. Drugs have little place in this narrative: nobody in the British press—and there are numerous reports of the murder—has yet alluded to the drug angle in any significant manner.

Perhaps this wouldn't have mattered to me if I hadn't myself been Indian.

Coming back to Bombay is like a short trip back from loonyland to certainty, until that illusion too is punctured. In Bombay, I head towards the CBI headquarters, looking for the answers I never found in Goa. Inspector Panicker, a paunchy Malayali who had investigated the Kelly case, sits across from me, his lips locked into a delicate silence. Panicker is clearly dying to discuss the case, but can't do so without permission from his superiors. But India

has a long and colourful history spanning centuries of circum-
vention. Gathering strength from this tradition, Panicker points
me in the direction of the Esplanade court house at Dhobitalao,
'where you will find as public records everything that I cannot
say.' He gives me the file number, 12/92, without which I would
never have found the file, and helpfully sends along a constable to
ensure that I do find everything he cannot say.

If file 12/92 is to be believed, Henry and Jerry Serrao are
guilty beyond a shred of doubt.

Everything in the file shrieks GUILTY—background (*matka,*
street fights, Jerry's prior arrest for breaking into a house in Mapusa);
testimony (Jerry always carries a folding knife, the weapon used
to slit Kelly's throat); witnesses (who tell how they saw Jerry with
large sums of money and a camera, and how they helped Jerry
wash a blood-stained jacket at their house around the time of the
murder); his own behaviour (he runs away from Goa right after
the murder and is arrested in Gujarat under the name of Jerry
Dias). Jerry's own confession, recorded in chilling detail right
from the logistical arrangements for the killing to the entry into
Kelly's room, the two brothers dressed as waiters, is the final nail
in his coffin.

File 12/92 seems to contain everything needed to convict
Jerry and Henry, *except the motive.* But even without the motive, I
am convinced of their guilt. My doubts are put to rest. I am whole-
heartedly on Paul Kelly's side. I rush back to CBI headquarters.

'This was not a robbery,' says Panicker. 'There has to be a
stronger motive for this kind of killing.'

'So what if there is no motive,' I argue, 'Isn't his confession
enough to convict Henry and Jerry?'

'Forget the confession,' says Panicker abruptly, as if it's im-
material. 'I have never used third-degree on anyone as I used on
them. Never.'

I can't believe what I'm hearing: is Panicker saying the confession was forced out of them, and amounts to nothing?

'Anyway, Jerry's statement is inadmissible in an Indian court without supporting evidence,' continues Panicker.

'Why?' I ask, completely bewildered by now.

'Because all Indians are *chootiyas*. They'll use force to get untrue confessions.'

'But what about the other stuff in the file?' I demand, determined to force his hand. I want answers—yes, no, innocent, guilty; I'm tired of being stuck in no-man's land.

'Oh, we just wrote all that to get remand,' says Panicker, dismissing a fileful of evidence with a wave of his hand. 'I'm telling you all this only because you are Indian. If you were British, I would not tell you.'

By the time I reach the Serrao household, I am ready to collapse with frustration; I'm certainly not ready to deal with hysteria. 'Kill my sons,' screams Sarah Serrao, mother of Jerry and Henry. 'Kill my sons if they killed a man. Throw them into the sea.' Sarah, a tiny woman with a big voice, staunchly stands by her sons' innocence. 'When they find the real culprit, I will be the first to hit him.'

Meeting Sarah Serrao is a painfully dissonant experience. Her body is that of a wispy ten-year old, but her face is the wizened face of a widow who has gone through troubled times. Her talk is that of a mother—'How will I marry my sons off after all this?'—but her language is the rough argot of a gangster's moll. 'Who the fuck does the CBI think they are!' We sit on Sarah's 'bed', a tiny wooden trunk in the corridor of the house where she works as a domestic. And as she drifts incoherently, seamlessly, from one thing to another, I get, for the first time in my research, a sense of real pain—and helplessness. Pain that her sons are involved, I idly wonder, or pain that they aren't and have had to go through all this?

If Sarah is a study in pain, Henry is rage. Pure, unalloyed rage. He has already checked my antecedents with the CBI before I

meet him; the distance between police and thieves is obviously
not as wide as assumed. All Henry's pent-up rage is directed at the
CBI. 'I know where they live,' he says. 'I know how they come to
work. I will get my own back on them.' Another dissonant moment
for me. Are these the inchoate rantings of a hot-headed criminal,
angry at being caught, or the helpless rage of an innocent man,
unjustly accused?

My mind flashes back to a torn sheet of paper neatly tucked
away in file 12/92. 'We both brothers are innocent in the name of
God and we were told by the CBI officers that we are innocent,'
the paper read. 'In spite of the law knowing we are innocent, it
does injustice to us. We will never forgive anybody in this world
and we will be forced to become criminals all our life.' It was
signed by Henry Serrao.

This is a turning point in the Kelly murder case, for me.
Until now, I have merely skirted the issue: chasing goombas and
softening up witnesses to appear on TV. This is the first time I
have come face to face with someone directly accused of the
murder. Suddenly I am forced to confront the fact that what is
just a television story for me may be a matter of life and death
for them. Correspondingly, I notice, the story has shifted in my
head. I'm not investigating 'Who killed Raymond Kelly?'
anymore. I'm investigating another story of my own making:
'Are the Serraos guilty or innocent?' This is a crucial story for
me, for if the Serraos are indeed innocent, do I have the right to
hang them on television?

As usual, I carry my moral dilemma to Mark. But Mark is
on a totally different wavelength now, as the TV programme
moves closer to the reality of being made. Cheers! he whoops,
completely jubilant that I have tracked down the Serraos and
am on such good terms with them. Mark outlines how he plans
to use the Serraos on TV. In essence, they will be softened up
with a few polite questions, and then voila, Paul Kelly will be
sprung on them. This will provide the climax of the show; a

massive 'live' confrontation between the dead man's brother-avenger and his killers—real-life packaged as television drama.

I am explicitly told not to warn the Serraos of the impending confrontation. But by now, my loyalties are beginning to swing wildly, and I feel a great sense of discomfort. All said and done, Mark is just a disembodied voice on the phone for me; Sarah and Henry are real people whom I have met—and empathized with. They are much more real to me than the dead man. I feel like our paths are diverging. While Mark's concern is still the television programme he is making, my concern has suddenly switched to real life.

Before he hangs up, Mark asks me to follow one more lead, an innocuous little detail that has got buried in the mountain of evidence: Prakash Naik, the room boy at Nova Goa who took breakfast up to the dead man. A bloodstained shirt and hotel bedsheet were found in his locker, recalls Mark. His testimony may tie the Serraos into the murder, he says, trying to assuage my doubts. The shirt will be sent to London for DNA testing—if the blood on it is Raymond Kelly's, it will conclusively tie Prakash, and through him the Serraos, to the murder.

Although this is a matter of life and death for the Serrao brothers and Prakash, I am told not to warn them of the possibility of DNA testing. I consider this grossly unethical.

Back to Goa, one more time, for a quest that is now as much a personal need as a professional obligation. If I can establish that the Serraos are guilty, maybe I won't feel so bad about letting Kelly confront them. A moral dilemma. Can it be resolved by the truth?

Strangely enough, my quest for Prakash takes me back to the Nova Goa hotel in Panjim, where it all began. A helpful manager gives me his address in an obscure village in old Goa, the area known as Goa Velha. I drive through narrow village lanes past palm trees, women washing vessels, a steaming train in the distance. At one point, I stop to ask a young man the way. A thin dark lad in his twenties with a nervous twitch. 'Straight ahead, straight ahead,' he points. I drive up and down that palm-fringed lane a dozen times, without locating Prakash.

Finally, I see our twitching friend heading our way and flag him down. Offering to show the way, he gets into the Maruti van. Soon, we pull into the courtyard of a small house. A bunch of women gather curiously around the vehicle. Our friend leads us through the crowd into a small two-roomed house. He goes inside, locks the door behind him and turns around to face me. 'I am Prakash,' he says.

It takes me almost half an hour to convince Prakash I have not come to arrest him. He is completely distraught and can barely talk. I have to handle him like an infant, gently soothing him by rhythmically repeating the same story again and again. His hands are trembling so much he looks like a man who has lost all motor control. And his story, when it dribbles out in bits and pieces, is impossible to follow.

One truth appears above all others at this point—this man should not appear on the programme.

My belief is based on my understanding of what I see of Prakash. All said and done, he is just a poor Goan villager whose life has already been destroyed by the Kelly murder. He quit the hotel shortly after the murder and hasn't been able to get a job after that. He can't stop his hands from shaking; his wrist is thinner than that of a baby. He is barely alive in any meaningful sense. What will he be after a TV interview?

I suddenly see it all very clearly. My Maruti van has already attracted enough attention in this quiet village; what will it be like with foreigners, boom mikes, cameras and all? How will Prakash deal with a hostile Kelly, when he can barely talk to me? Suppose the TV programme succeeds beyond its intentions—the shirt is DNA-tested, establishing Prakash's involvement. He doesn't even know this is possible. How can he protect himself against it?

Let him live his quiet life by the river, I say.

At this point, I step out of the picture. I don't care any more whether the Serraos killed Raymond. Or whether Prakash Naik helped them in anyway. Whatever the truth, I don't want them to be lynched, by television at least.

And it will be lynching; have no doubt. Is the camera ever objective? Are audiences ever really neutral? Picture the scene. A British crew, with little concern for or empathy with the Serraos. Paul Kelly, suave, English-speaking, a representative of the law. On the other hand, the Serraos: Sarah, rambling, foul-mouthed, the blue tattoo on her arm damning her more than any abuses she could heap on Paul Henry, inarticulate with rage, stammering incoherently, ungrammatically in pidgin English. Prakash can't even speak English, he will be subtitled.

I have long crossed the invisible boundaries that separate journalist and human being, professional and personal, objectivity and emotion, crime and punishment. I stop taking notes. I don't care any more who killed Raymond Kelly. All conventional signposts of morality have dissolved into a landscape of greys where there is no right, no wrong, no good, no bad, no truth, no lies.

Instinctively, I feel the Serraos are involved in the murder—but I'm on their side. I always thought murder was an absolute; if you met a murderer, you would 'naturally' be against him. Now it just seems relative, like everything else in the world. What does it mean when you start out wanting to find the murderers and end up wanting to defend them? I don't know.

All know is this: I don't want to be part of Paul Kelly's revenge.

One month after I have taken on the Kelly assignment, I unhappily resign. But the tale turns out to have a happy ending after all, at least from my point of view. The Indian government denies the television company a permit to film in India. The programme is never made. To this day, nobody knows what happened in room 203.

(June 1996)

PANKAJ MISHRA

Among the Believers

'Sonia, God loves you. Sonia, Goa loves you.' It was what the banners and freshly painted billboards on the road from the airport said ('God' always looking like a likely spelling mistake), but they were the only sign, until the day it happened, of Mrs Gandhi's visit. Where were the outlandish cut-outs, the loudspeaker jeeps, the goons with bullhorns?

'I have only a widow,' the hapless Sitaram Kesri had blurted out to an interviewer soon after Sonia Gandhi finally agreed to do her bit for the beleaguered party of her husband and mother-in-law. I read the interview in Goa, and it didn't seem then as if the widow was being put to good use. What, for instance, was she expected to achieve in Goa, an early stop on her campaign tour? Corruption may yet again be the leitmotif of Lok Sabha elections, but the issues in Goa remain strictly local. People talk in worried tones about the fragile condition of one of the bridges that links the airport to the beaches in the northern part of the state—one of the arterial bridges in the state collapsed a few years ago. Other expend their political energy over the tourist shacks on the beaches that the government wants to remove.

So when I asked Goans about Mrs Gandhi's visit, they appeared surprised; and then wondered why she was coming.

After all, Goa had only two seats out of 525 in the Lok Sabha. Calmly cynical in his air-conditioned cabin, the journalist offered what seemed like an explanation rolled up inside a theory: Sonia Gandhi, he said, was still testing the waters in these early days of her campaign and her tour organizers had chosen Goa because as a 'white-skinned' Catholic from a Mediterranean country she might have a good chance of attracting large crowds in the state.

He said, 'The Goans have a weakness for white-skinned people. They miss the Portuguese chaps who ruled them for four centuries, and they now spend all their unused devotion on British and German tourists. But you see', he smiled, 'the comedy of the situation is that the poor woman wants nothing more than to persuade voters that she is hundred per cent Indian.'

Panjim, Goa's capital, is a small coastal town with elegant old balconeyed houses leaning over narrow alleys and white-washed churches overlooking large leafy squares. It is not built to accommodate crowds, and early on the morning of Mrs Gandhi's visit its complicated traffic system of one-way streets became quickly congested with buses hired to bring in people from nearby rural areas. The buses—ramshackle after years on pot-holed rural roads—were many, and enthusiastically blared their horns as they inched their way to the meeting venue.

But few of them carried more than nine or ten passengers, the passengers themselves looking rather forlorn as they listlessly held paper Congress flags and anxiously peered out into the streets where smartly attired groups of traffic policemen (Goa is probably the only state where the police wear designer uniforms) flailed their arms and blew shrill whistles.

At the meeting venue (smaller than the venue for a middle-class Punjabi wedding and chosen, one heard, after the organizers grew nervous about filling up any of the larger grounds in the city) there were spare seats going at even 11 a.m., the time for the scheduled start of the meeting. Outside, policemen stood idle in small groups, easily outnumbering everyone else present there. Curious passers-by stopped and gawked. A couple of over-tanned British tourists who looked as if they had strayed into town from one of the beaches in the north frantically took pictures of the cows in the adjacent street.

Inside, under the colourful shamiana that had been put up to shade the audience from the harsh Goan sun, boredom hung heavy in the air. On one side of the podium, a local group of singers intoned 'Rajiv Gandhi *amar rahe,* Sonia Gandhi *amar rahe,* Jawaharlal Nehru *amar rahe'* in the mechanical manner of a *purohit* reciting the *Ram Charita Manas.* An occasional 'Mahatma Gandhi *amar rahe'* was also heard—a token bow to the original Gandhi, who, since he did not belong to the dynasty, tends to be left out on such occasions.

Most local members of the crowd looked to be taking their afternoon siestas on their chairs. Only the tribal women in their starched white sarees looked reasonably alert, quietly enjoying as they were their good fortune: they had been transported *en masse* earlier in the morning from neighbouring Maharashtra, at a rate of Rs 50 cash and a saree each. (The woman who told me this hadn't previously heard of Sonia Gandhi.) Sewa Dal volunteers resembling, in their white Gandhi caps and shirts with epaulettes, cabin boys on an improbable Gandhian cruise-liner, stood with arms crossed across chest and cast vacant glances around the shamiana, until they spied the bored TV cameraman in purple bicycle shorts aiming a long snout in their direction and suddenly stiffened to attention. Travel-weary journalists from Europe leaned against the ropes that separated the audience from the podium thirty metres away, and thought of, probably, a hot shower and clean sheets. The Italian photographers quietly screwed and unscrewed long lenses on their cameras.

It was into these soporific environs that the Youth Congress cadres infused a malevolent energy—the dingy anteroom to main-stream politics once again living up to its reputation. Wearing white bandannas with the revised YC logo, and shouting incoherent slogans, they shoved and pushed their way to the front of the press enclosure. It was a most un-Goan display of aggressiveness, and it incited dark allusions among the assembled crowd to 'Congress culture'. Angry voices were raised; a few arguments broke out. The journalists craned their necks to see Mario Cabral, Goa's resident writer, loudly remonstrating with a corpulent YC activist. 'Throw out the *chamcha!*' a journalist cried. The crowd broke into assenting cheers.

But then the motorcade sirens were heard, and everyone's attention turned to the far side of the podium, where there was a flurry of activity among the various white-clad, paunchy Congressmen. In a matter of seconds, they had lined up like obedient schoolboys to be introduced to Sonia Gandhi who barely looked at them as she nodded and shook their hands. Sections of the crowd began to shout slogans at uncoordinated intervals. Sensing their moment, the singers began to sing even more loudly, producing a lot of crackle on the PA system, as Mrs Gandhi proceeded towards the podium. But most of the audience was busy scanning Mrs Gandhi's entourage—the assortment of security men and the family's permanent hangers-on—for signs of Priyanka, whose two badly pronounced words in Tamil had sent the crowd at an earlier rally into raptures.

But Priyanka wasn't here today, and the absence of her convent-headgirl prettiness only forced into greater relief the essential fact about Sonia Gandhi: her near total lack of charisma.

She walks fast, looking neither left nor right but fixedly ahead; it is the unnatural briskness of someone who cannot but be perpetually alive to the possibility that among the friendly-seeming crowd may lurk a suicide bomber of the kind that killed her unsuspecting husband. The saree today is an elegant beige, suitable for one of those tea parties on the lawns of the presidential palace Mrs Gandhi is frequently photographed at: she hasn't inherited her mother-in-law's instinct in these matters (expensive silks for appearances at the White House, simple handlooms for tribal areas, head demurely covered).

She emerges on the podium, raises her hand and waves, thus exposing the sweat patch on her armpit, which, visible in press pictures of her other rallies, has grown larger in Goa's moist heat. A smile tries to break out of the broad alabaster-complexioned face with small eyes. But the hand moves within a rigidly determined arc; the wave is too clearly something acquired from the repertoire of her late husband's crowd-pleasing gestures. The smile has no warmth; the face remains steadfastly immune to expression. Unique among all election campaigners in the world, Mrs Gandhi barely glances at the journalists quietly agog in one corner of the audience.

Then it is time for the introductory speeches, and she settles back in her chair with a thick manuscript on her lap. The tone of introductory speeches was set in Tamil Nadu, where Mrs Gandhi was greeted by the president of the local Congress Committee with the following words: 'I prostrate before thee, oh mother, lead the Congress, lead the country, lead us.' As everyone knows, they tend to overdo this kind of thing in Tamil Nadu, but the first speaker here—the president of the Goa Pradesh Congress Committee, a little man wearing a safari suit and a Hitler-like moustache—is determined not to come second best in the unctuousness stakes. The journalists titter and snap shut their notebooks as he walks up to the podium.

'Madam', he begins, 'it gives me great pleasure to welcome you to the tiny land of Goa.' A potted history of the Nehru-Gandhi affection for Goa now follows. 'Madam, Nehru freed us from the bondage of 450 years'—the Catholics in the crowd murmur resentfully. 'Madam, your husband, Shri Rajiv Gandhiji gave statehood to Goa on a platter'. This raises some frank laughter at the back but he is only warming up to his theme. 'Madam, you are the torch bearer of secularism, the inheritor of the Nehru-Gandhi legacy. Madam, you have electrified the country with your campaign. Madam, you now have to guide world's largest democracy. Madam', he ends with an abruptly loud exhortation, 'Goa is with you, Goans are with you.'

But Madam has long given up on him, and is correcting her speech in consultation with Rane, the chief minister, who by placing himself between Mrs Gandhi and his rival, De Souza, the deputy CM, has foreclosed all possibility of any conversation between them. (Much entertainment is provided for Goans by the exchange of creative insults between the chief minister and De Souza, a portly old Catholic surgeon. The papers next day were to report that Sonia Gandhi's election meeting opened with the latest instalment of their ongoing feud. De Souza arrived at the venue to find no seat for him on the podium. 'Insult! Humiliation!' muttered his supporters, and threatened a 'walkout' before another chair was hurriedly placed on the podium.)

Rane speaks for a while in Konkani, as De Souza, who is not one of the speakers, sullenly looks on. Then it is Mrs Gandhi's turn, and the journalist sitting next to me turns to a fresh page in his notebook and carefully writes on the top: Sonia!

The exclamation mark was to seem a bit optimistic later on. The day before in Hyderabad, Mrs Gandhi had launched her first frontal attack on the BJP; it was a carefully timed sop to her largely Muslim audience. Accordingly, she begins with some specially chosen words for the people of Goa, who are told that the rest of India 'admires' their 'achievement'—it is not clear in what area. Goa's 'sunny beaches' and 'vibrant culture' are referred to before she moves on to the confessional stuff: 'My grief and loss have been deeply personal ... but the time has come to put duty before personal consideration ... to fight narrow and selfish interests.'

Written in correct if formal English, the speech is already an over-rehearsed routine, having not changed in any substantial way since she first went on the campaign trail. It makes little reference to the forthcoming elections; the parliamentary candidates for Goa are, inexplicably, not even mentioned—after the meeting a tall man in trendy dark glasses went around telling anyone who listened to him that he was the 'official candidate'. It presses all the right buttons; plucks at emotional strings still resonating from the time Indira and Rajiv Gandhi tugged at them. It addresses the question of her allegiance to India with a mixture of populist melodrama and recent history ('my husband and mother-in-law sacrificed their lives for the country'). It does everything it possibly can. Yet the overall effect remains unimpressive. It is partly because Sonia Gandhi cannot but affirm her 'unwavering and absolute' commitment to India in a very foreign-sounding voice that furthermore rarely fluctuates beyond a monotonous drone. The accent is unmistakably Italian: the *ts* and *ds* are soft throughout, and concern is pronounced 'coancern'. They make it even hard to escape the sense that she has let herself be persuaded into a false position by the hundreds of Congressmen trampling over her front garden every morning.

The unenthused crowd, 5,000 strong by now, goes through its own motions; all the determined prodding by full-throated cheerleaders—the corpulent Youth Congress activist is an especially frenzied figure—only results in a few feeble cheers. The journalists slowly close their notebooks as Mrs Gandhi begins to speak of the need to 'nurture excellence in science and industry'. Eyes swivel upwards and around to follow the Black Cat commandos pacing the top storeys of the buildings overlooking the park as Mrs Gandhi goes on about how much her husband wanted to prepare India for the twenty-first century. Suddenly, it all has a drearily over-familiar ring. We have drifted back into *Mera Bharat Mahaan* territory.

As it turned out, the speech was Mrs Gandhi's shortest so far, but some people had begun to leave even as it ran out of platitudes. And after it ended and she departed from the venue—for the Governor's residence, where posed pictures of her looking unhappy with the chief minister's extended family were to appear in the next day's papers—the crowd was quick to disperse. In just a few minutes, the park was virtually empty, and the fresh posses of policemen arranged to deal with the possibility of stampedes looked as underused and idle as their colleagues in the morning. Only the villagers and the tribal women brought in hired buses stayed put, and they were still there an hour later, abandoned, the buses standing empty outside the secretariat, their drivers waiting, someone suggested, to be paid by the Congressmen inside the building.

Later, I ran into an Italian journalist I knew. He was following Sonia Gandhi's campaign tour across South India, and he had been careful not to let the complexities of Indian politics, or indeed Mrs Gandhi's refusal to speak to the media, get in his way. He already had his story; and was surprised that I didn't have mine. Sonia Gandhi was big news in Italy, but it wasn't her politics anyone was interested in. It was the other stuff.

'What's the English word? Yes, soap-opera. Here is the story so far: Lower-middle-class family makes it big in the 1950s economic boom—you have already got millions of Italians tuning in. Pretty daughter of the house goes to Cambridge to learn English. Meets dark and handsome Indian prince; falls in love. They marry, have two attractive children. But tragedy stalks the prince's family. His younger brother, the emperor-elect, is killed in an air crash. Then his mother, the empress of India, is murdered. The prince is called upon by the dynasty's loyal subjects to step into her role. His wife "fights like a tigress" to stop him from doing so, but fails. He, the great visionary, wants to lead India into the twenty-first century, but tragedy again intervenes, and he, too, is assassinated. The Italian widow retreats into private grief, and then emerges seven years later to lead the party of her husband and mother-in-law to—well, nobody knows what will happen now, but you have to grant me this: even Oriana Fallaci couldn't have thought up a plot where a middle-class woman from near Torino tries to rescue India's oldest political party from extinction.'

I felt I had to grant him that.

(February 1998)

MUKUL KESAVAN

Hinterland

Elections are occasions for urban travelogues on the other India. Of the five assembly segments that make up the Lucknow Lok Sabha constituency, Mohona is the only one that's rural. Nabeel lives here. Since real people don't live in the categories of the Election Commission, he actually lives in Mauza Palamau, a village an hour's walk from the railway line which formally divides Lucknow's Gomti Nagar (and, by extension, urban India) from the great Indian hinterland. I thought the rail line was a touch obvious; some less predictable metaphor should have been found, but you can't argue with the real world, which is sometimes not as subtle as it ought to be.

Anyway, we crossed the track because it was there, and began walking. It was 5.30 and the light was beginning to go. Ajit and I had flown into Lucknow around lunch time and till we began walking towards Mauza Palamau our day had been ordinarily urban. We had eaten three breakfasts, the first of which we bought at Palam because Modiluft cancelled our flight; we then realized that the airline was serving one free, so we ate that too, and completed the treble on the Indian Airlines plane to which we had been transferred. In the taxi from Lucknow airport we saw an ancient Congressman walking doggedly along the side of the road, with a large tricolour on his shoulder and while Ajit committed him to memory to sketch him later, I did the prescribed, time-honoured thing and asked the taxi driver who he thought would win the elections. We found rooms without difficulty at the Carlton, which wasn't surprising since it looked and functioned like a nineteenth-century ruin. It was still an atmospheric building, but too decrepit and dysfunctional to be attractive. Like the Congress . . . it just was one of those metaphoric days.

For a couple of hours we talked to journalists, rang up party offices, called on the BJP, all of which left us feeling superficial and conventional and inauthentic and disconnected from India, which lives in its villages. So when Nabeel, who I know from a previous visit, agreed to take us to his village, the effect on us was electric; we felt plugged in. This was a mistake: we set out looking for the real India and found ourselves in foreign parts. '*Dehaat* is another country,' as L.P. Hartley once nearly wrote, 'they do things differently over there.'

We travelled to the limits of the city in a Vikram, Lucknow's all-purpose substitute for the three-wheeler, the phut-phut and the taxi. It set us down at the railway line where the strangeness began at once. As we crossed the track, Nabeel drew our attention to an exploded buffalo lying unevenly broadcast over the rail lines some thirty feet from us. Ajit and I would have missed it altogether, partly because we were unused to rural life and its sights and sounds, but also because the animal had depreciated since its death. A panchayat of patient vultures was inspecting the leftovers more closely than we were. Nabeel wanted to take us nearer the scene but we declined. There were, I thought, lessons to be learnt from this simple tableau, this passing glimpse of the rural scene. Some were straightforward. No buffalo could hope to derail a train. But more largely, it brought to mind the unequal contest between tradition and modernity and the bludgeoning passage of the Modern Juggernaut over the carcass of the Past.

Not all the metaphors this sight inspired were melancholy. It was heartening to see these secular birds go about their scavenging task without once worrying whether the meat was *jhatka* or *halal*, eating the buffalo on an as-is-where-is basis, careless of caste and creed. 'Just like Malayalees,' said Ajit grinning. 'We eat a lot of beef in Kerala.'

What Nabeel wanted to show us was different. The stuff on the tracks wasn't all buffalo meat; there were lots of quartered vultures in there too. The greedy birds had been run over while feeding, by a later train. 'Idiots,' said Nabeel contemptuously. After this, and after we slid down the embankment, the spell broke, the metaphors dried up and our surroundings became more matter of fact. The terrain was pointlessly undulating; it did nothing for the landscape, it simply made walking more difficult. After fifteen minutes of reasonably brisk trudging we still hadn't left the vultures behind. There were clumps of them everywhere. Some of them would suddenly take to the air and then sit down again. The interior of Columbia is nothing compared to the rural suburbs of Lucknow, I thought. The best Marquez can do is swarms of butterflies and here we are, within earshot of Lucknow, already walking beneath a sky hung with vultures.

For nearly an hour we walked through uncultivated land. Nabeel explained that most of it had been sold to urban speculators so no one sowed there anymore. Then suddenly, our surroundings turned into fields, some green, others piled with neat brown stacks of harvested wheat. We walked past villages, some Yadav, some Muslim, where Nabeel knew everyone or seemed to. He asked everyone he passed if they had harvested and they asked him the same question. He had. He owned three *bighas* in three separate fields. There had been more land once but three *bighas* was all there was left, so he also worked on building sites in the city. He liked whitewashing houses.

I noticed that the Yadav villages were brilliant with violently

coloured domes and *shikhars*. I asked Nabeel about these. They
were temples, he said. The people who had come into money by
selling their fields as urban real estate invariably used a part of it to
build a temple. The spires, painted gold and blue and purple and
orange, were bizarrely beautiful in the twilight where everything
else had faded to greys and browns and dying greens. We passed a
temple flag on the right planted in the middle of nowhere. Nabeel
pointed to a settlement on our left. It was a Yadav village. A monkey
from Nabeel's village had migrated to the Yadav settlement and
died there, so they had buried him where the flag was and planned
to build a Hanuman temple there.

Did Yadavs and Muslims vote together? I asked carefully. He
shrugged. Sometimes, he said. Later, in his village, the *pradhan,* a
Muslim, said that during the last assembly election everyone in
Mohona, Yadav and Muslim alike, had voted for Mulayam's party.
They had returned a Yadav MLA. But this time the village's votes
would scatter because Mulayam's man had never once taken the
trouble to return. 'I didn't vote for Mulayam's party the last time
either,' Nabeel told me later. He hadn't liked Yadavs since the
Gomti changed course twenty years ago. The flooding river had
cut his field in half and when its course settled, most of his land
surfaced on the wrong bank of the river where the Yadavs claimed
it. As far as Nabeel was concerned, Mulayam had an elemental
problem.

Strangely for a man who made his living by helping build
houses, Nabeel hadn't one till recently, by which he meant a
proper house, a house he could lock. He had a respectable plot
of land in the village, walled off, with a door and a courtyard,
but it hadn't had a pukka roof or brick walls. Shelter for his
wife and five children had consisted of a *chhappar* or thatch
held up by bamboos. This presented practical problems. Most
simply the roof leaked in the monsoon and the children got
wet. But what worried Nabeel even more was the fact that the
family could never go out together for a wedding or an outing

to the city. Because before setting out they had to carry their pots and pans and any other portable belongings to his brother's house. They had done it a couple of times and then stopped because his wife felt shamed by the process. But last winter he had managed to put some money together and now they had a proper cement slab roof and brick walls. He had even put in metal door frames. Now all that remained were the doors. By the end of the year he would have enough money to pay for the wood. Then they'd lock the door and go to Gomti Nagar and see a film together.

Like Nabeel, the *pradhan* also built houses, but in a more exalted capacity. Nabeel worked as an unskilled labourer. The *pradhan* was a *rajmistry* a small contractor almost. He was helping raise many of the houses that city people were building in this part of Mohona. He did some real estate business on the side. Would we be interested in some land? he asked half-seriously. Land values were rising all the time.

Nobody seemed to think it odd that the head of the village was trying to sell it off in parcels to urban investors. Nabeel was clear-eyed about this; most of the fields were gone and more would go. When the prices went through his roof may be he would sell too and build another, better home for his family somewhere else.

It was dark now. Nabeel insisted on escorting us back to the railway line. We protested feebly but were glad of his company because it was so dark we couldn't see our feet. As we stumbled along behind him, he told us that the *pradhan* we had met wasn't actually the *pradhan*. The *pradhan's* post in his village was reserved by law for women. So each time elections came round, the men fielded their wives and the winner's husband became the de facto *pradhan*. Nothing in rural India was as it seemed to be. It wasn't even rural anymore; its title deeds were all in urban lockers. When we reached the railway track, the vultures had, like us, finished for the day. The buffalo, or what remained of it, was obscured by the dark. Ajit and I slipped Nabeel some money for the children, which he accepted unobsequiously. As we shook hands, he grinned and said: 'You've come a long way; you might as well tell me who to vote for before you go.'

(June 1996)

Message in a bottle

Indira Point on Great Nicobar Island is India's southern-most tip. If you look at the map, though, you wonder why Great Nicobar is a part of India at all. Strung out in the Bay of Bengal, much closer to Burma and Sumatra than to the Indian mainland, the Nicobar archipelago seems to have little to do with the rest of India.

On this furthest point, the sea dominates the land. The breeze is sticky with salt. The roar and hiss of the waves inhabits the mind in an ever-present echo. The light is mirror-bright as the ocean reflects the sun. The land itself has arisen from the sea— its mangrove swamps and coastal reefs are still shaping themselves to the tug of ocean tides. As you walk along the beach, leaving damp dimpled footprint tales on the coarse sand, and gaze out, the water is endless and you are alone.

Or are you?

Rustam Vania went to Great Nicobar to visit Ravi Sankaran. Rustam is an illustrator and environmental journalist. Ravi is a biologist studying the Nicobar megapode, a bird which looks rather like a hen but is remarkable for its habit of nesting like a reptile. The megapode is not found anywhere on the Indian subcontinent except Nicobar. It tends to lurk in the undergrowth of dense forest fringes and can also be spotted on the sandy seashore above the spring-tide mark. Since, in Rustam's experience, most biologists out in the wilderness have sketchy food arrangements, he took the precaution of including a packet of Maggi noodles in his rucksack.

At dusk, Ravi said what about food. Rustam made polite noises indicating not to bother, I have my Maggi. Ravi said no we must feed you. What will you have—lobster or fish? In a choked voice Rustam said lobster. Ravi called out Juglu! *Ek lobster le ao.* Assistant Juglu Mahanto picked up a torch and walked out to the tidal pool. Shone the torch and a pair of eyes gleamed in the dark. Juglu picked up the lobster and took it home. Then he shinned up a coconut tree and broke off a couple of coconuts with his hatchet. That night Rustam had lobster in coconut curry for dinner.

The next night the same question. Lobster or fish? Rustam said fish. Ravi called out Juglu! *Aaj fish khayenge.* Juglu picked up a torch and a spear and walked out to the tidal pool. Returned with a fish as long as a man's arm. Rustam was pleased, but everybody else groaned. Now we will have to eat fish for the next three days.

Lobster, coconuts, fish. The fruits of the sea.

In Ravi's home, Rustam Vania admired a chair improvized out of Styrofoam. Ravi said thank you. It came from the beach. He pointed to a large clothes basket. That came from the beach too. Ravi asked would you like to have a bath? Rustam said why not. Ravi brought him a bottle of shampoo, a foreign brand. And said that came from the beach. Then some aftershave. Also from the beach.

Ravi explained. The sea off Great Nicobar is heavily travelled. There is constant traffic along the trade route between Bombay and Penang. As the ships go to and fro beyond the horizon, they heave in their wake a stream of manufactured objects, tossed or swept off board. And the faithful tides deposit this bounty at the feet of the Nicobarese. Once a full-size refrigerator washed up like a beached whale at Indira Point.

When Rustam walked along the beach, he looked down and saw sea shells. He also saw bottles. Bisleri in a multitude of languages. Thai, French, Malay, Swedish, English. Mineral water bottled in Japan, Italy and Australia. Some glass beer bottles. Cans. Frooti-type cartons of juice, mango, grape, apple, even sake. The junk of the world.

After every storm, the Nicobarese are out in force. A treasure hunt is on at the beach, to spy out goodies to salvage and refurbish. No one knows about the Basel Convention on the import of toxic waste; they are already recycling the world's refuse.

Sunita Rao teaches environmental awareness in the Andaman and Nicobar Islands. She trains school teachers and has written a workbook on the subject. Sunita takes groups of schoolkids to the beach. Along with the wildlife they observe junk. Children squint with concentration trying to decipher the Thai or Japanese script. Between discussions—who throws things? why do they throw them? what can we do?—children amuse themselves by jumping on puffed-up Frooti packs and squashing them flat. Every tide brings in another lesson in political geography.

But the refuse of the world is not a novelty for the islanders. For hundreds of years, the people of the Onge tribe relied on the ocean to bring them their supply of iron. Washed up scrap metal— barrel hoops, nails embedded in planks of wood—would yield material for arrowheads. The arrows were not only for hunting; they held at bay foreign traders, settlers and conquerors. For the same sea that brought them the gifts of life could carry death to their shores. And the sea that cut them off from the rest of the world let that very world lap at their feet.

(May 1996)

Lost Valley

The 737 flew in low over stark, recently harvested fields, only just skimming above the stately poplars and chinars made gold and fire by the autumnal winds. Eight years since my last visit, eight years of war and change. The Kashmir of my childhood, the Kashmir of my imagination; I still don't know what connects me to it, why the feeling runs so deep. On the tarmac, under a slate-grey sky, just before entering the terminal I did something which, thinking about it later, embarrassed me no end. But then, at the moment under that sky with a chill wind in my hair, my bending over and scooping up a clod of earth and kissing it seemed no extravagant gesture.

Driving into Srinagar my very first impressions were to be reinforced later as the perfect referents for Kashmir, and so they remain in memory, indelibly etched: convoys of trucks carrying grim soldiers, armoured vehicles with LMGs sticking out of turrets, road blocks, bunkers, soldiers standing guard on street corners and then when you look beyond all of this: huge newly built houses, Swiss chalet-style, new Marutis and Zens on the roads, naked hills emptied of trees, garbage left uncollected on the streets . . . a signboard over a shop: Born Free Tailors.

Muzamil's flat, where I was to spend a lot of my three weeks, is in Jawahar Nagar, not far from Rajbagh and the river. He lives there with his mother, younger brothers Jami and Rafi, and three teenaged sisters Lucky, Kali and Farah. They meet me with warmth—as if we'd known one another for years.

The first couple of days I take it easy, absorb my surroundings, drink endless cups of tea, go for walks along the Jhelum under magnificent chinars. The Dal lake looks wan and a little neglected. We go for a *shikara* ride anyway and I am flooded with memories of a long-ago childhood: we are distraught because the little rubber ball has bounced off the edge of the houseboat's roof and into the water, until an old man glides up out of nowhere in his boat and returns it to us. Then the water had seemed clear, good enough to go swimming in if only our parents would let us. Now the route through the famous Lotus Garden is choked with weeds, houseboats lie forlornly under weeping willows even as the *shikara*walla tells me that tourism has been better this year after a long time. I see one or two white men in a houseboat far away.

The only other *shikaras* about have BSF men with automatic rifles patrolling the Dal. They get angry and shout when I pick up my camera to photograph. Bunkers crouch under nets at every corner, the hotels on the Boulevard and Bund are occupied by the forces with the tell-tale sign of uniforms drying outside every window.

It is still lovely by the lake. We sip tea, eat hot *kanti kababs* from a roadside vendor. At dusk the sky looks huge and watery as if the land below were not land but sea, or maybe reclaimed land. The air is soft, the colours delicate pastels or faded flowers. A land made for love, for poetry, for great learning. For the third Buddhist Council, for Zail-ul Abidin, for Bulbul Shah and his beard where the little birds are said to have nested in peace, for the love songs of Habba Khatoon and the *vaakh* of Lalla, for the meditations of Noor-ud-din Wali and the *ibaadat* of Maqdoom sahab, for moonlit picnics in Nishat . . .

The guns and steel and cold faces and cold hearts sit uncomfortably in this lambent landscape, which makes me think that perhaps in this long narrative the present age is only a short parentheses, a short parentheses for small characters to play out their bit roles. How else can one describe the fevered outpourings of the nationalists, or for that matter, the fervors of the sub-nationalist?

It is in this mood that I argued with Muzamil's mother one evening. We were all sitting around before dinner, legs tucked into blankets, when someone said something about dying for one's country. I said to die for a cause was one of the most banal forms of heroism and that dying for a nation was the most unimaginative of them all. Besides, it's never the architects of such plans who die but the innocents, the hot-blooded fools who trust in them. And then Behenji, leaning against the wall, said, 'It's all Allah's will anyway.'

'What? 40,000 dead and you say it's Allah's will?' I asked, incredulous.

We argue hotly for a while.

'It's not enough to talk of God's will or *kismat* or whatever. The day people own responsibility for their actions the world would be a saner place to live in. The Allah that I know from my childhood is the merciful and compassionate, strange how we attribute our follies to him,' I try and explain, but she shakes her head obdurately. 'Without Allah's will a leaf can't tremble in the breeze. And remember great causes require great sacrifices.'

I start despairing at this glorifying of war. Jami joins in and speaks of sin and retribution, of the Kashmiri people paying for past sins.

'So you're being punished?'

'Yes.'

'So how can you call this a Jihad with Allah's sanction or all the dead martyrs, then?'

By the time dinner is served I'm not hungry anymore. Sitting in a corner I stare into a book. They turn to me one by one, 'Didi, *bata khao* . . . Didi's angry with us,' they giggle, 'she won't eat.'

'Sonia ji,' Muzamil's mother comes to me, eyes twinkling, cupping my face in both her hands with infinite tenderness, 'Come child . . . eat.' I grin, feeling a bit silly, and then tuck into a mound of rice, *haak* and fatty meat. We laugh together and shake our heads.

Then there are long days filled with meetings. First to Yaseen Malik's house in Maisuma, where we are met warmly by Javed Mir, one of the first to have advocated the armed struggle. We are ushered into a tiny blue room. The house is old and the walls are made of mud so it is warm inside on this cold October morning. Yaseen's sister brings a flask of *kehva* and plates of assorted Kashmiri breads and biscuits. Everywhere we go the warmth and hospitality is generous, heartfelt.

Later someone tells me stories about this family: of this sister's divorce because her husband couldn't stay married into a militant's family, of the younger sister, stunningly beautiful, articulate, who remains single; of his father, who still drives trucks between Srinagar and Leh, of the mother, like so many Kashmiri mothers, tempered by long anxious nights of waiting for her son to return. Yaseen enters looking worn out and frail. We have met intermittently in these last few years and there is a curious affection between us even though our politics differ. Once, I remember, after a long argument, he had pulled my rather pliable thumb all the way back until it nearly touched my wrist. 'See, I knew it!' he said triumphantly, 'You are weak, exhausted, unable to comprehend revolutions.' 'No, you're wrong again,' I said, 'it's just that my hand isn't able to do this very easily,' and I curled my fingers into a fist.

Later I go to the secretariat to meet the Minister for Social Welfare, Mian Altaf. The security is incredible, like hundreds of fine-toothed combs that you have to pass through. I begin to feel sorry for the people who have to work here. The minister is generous with his time and seems eager to get work done, but

there are insurmountable problems for this unpopular government. Nonetheless we talk about the Rehabilitation Council
set up by the government some ten months ago.

I was particularly interested in this project because it indicated
a step in the right direction. Presently anyone even indirectly
involved in militancy or the *azaadi* movement is automatically
disqualified from any claims to compensation. So women, for
example, who may not have supported militancy but lost husbands
or sons who were militants found themselves bereft of state support.
There are an estimated 30,000 such cases. The council proposed
not to discriminate between cases and to set up funds for widows,
orphans and amputees. This would not only go a long way in
rebuilding lives which have been utterly devastated by the war
but also, perhaps, be perceived by the Kashmiris as a gesture towards
reconciliation.

The minister and director of the council elaborate. What
emerges is a picture of absolute inertness: nothing has been done
so far. They are waiting to collect a corpus fund of twenty crores
before they can start. For the uninitiated, a corpus fund is something that the J&K government would invest in a bank and use
only the interest gained for this project. I'm no economist or
planner but this seemed an absurd way of bringing relief to a
people that needed it immediately. I voice my concerns. The director shrugs and spreads his hands out in a gesture of helplessness. 'We have already collected six and a half crores and we're
waiting for New Delhi to release an equivalent amount.'

'Then why can't you start with what you already have? Surely
it would be politically expedient for you?' I am answered with
the same ineffectual gesture.

At the Hurriyat office I am invited to join them for lunch.
We sit in a circle on the floor, the silence broken only by the
sucking of rice into wizened old mouths. I find myself tense
and unable to eat more than what I force down. Across me sits
Yaseen, not looking at me or speaking. Next to him sits the

young Mirwaiz, Umar Farooq, looking broader and more filled out than the slight, unsure boy I have seen in photographs. It is he who breaks the silence and asks Yaseen about me. He replies in Kashmiri and gives me an opportunity to joke and cut the ice: 'You'd better speak in Urdu or English, I don't trust what you say about me.'

Later a bunch of Kashmiri friends substantiate the strange feeling of squeamishness that I'd carried around all afternoon. That evening, in a small smoky office with an electric heater warming us, I hear stories about the grand old leaders of the various political parties that have come together on the platform called the All Parties Hurriyat Conference, who claim to represent the interests of the people of Kashmir. Stories of the amassing of incredible wealth, of terrible corruption; of the cold and systematic elimination of rival groups.

Difficult to believe these rumours, they seem so incredible, but even more difficult to verify them. But all I know is that the scores of Kashmiri people I spoke with at length throughout my stay believe them to be true, and that it is simply impossible for them therefore to regard the Hurriyat as a solution to the present crisis.

I am driving a borrowed white Maruti down the poplar-lined Baramulla highway heading north from Srinagar. Muzamil wears his cheap Italian rainbow sunglasses which he claims cost him $300. I tell him it looks more like a Bangkok rip-off and he more like a Delhi puppie. He accuses me of being an Indian agent. We are both high on the bright sunny weather and landscape we drive through. We laugh easily. He sings off-key to a song in the tape player, a track from *Border* which I'd found quite silly in the film, but here in this land it takes on a peculiar poignancy, '*mere dushman, mere bhai, mere husaye . . . tera bhi vatan, mera bhi vatan,*' so I find myself humming along. Ahead we catch up with a convoy of army trucks. 'Slow down and don't, for God's sake, overtake.'

'Why?' He gives me a look. This question was to become a great source of irritation to him in the days to come. 'Just do it okay ... and listen, if you see a convoy coming from the opposite side slow down, move right over. Okay?'

'Okay.'

The vehicles slow down and turn off into an encampment and we both relax. The road winds slowly through apple orchards. It is beautiful. '*Sandese aate hain hume tarpate hain ki ghar kab aaoge, likho kab aaoge,*' we sing happily. After a little while I see a convoy approaching from the other side. I follow instructions and slow to 40 kmph and hug the shoulder of the road. As we come closer I see each truck has a soldier in a black bandanna shouldering a Light Machine Gun mounted on the cab. As the distance between us closes I realize that the leading truck starts to move from the centre of the road closer to my side. 'What? What's he doing?' I grow alarmed and try and shrink even further. At the moment we cross I see a soldier lean right out of the truck and swing a staff at us. There is a resounding crash on the roof which makes me leap out of my skin. 'What?! Bastard. What did he do that for?!' Before I can say or do anything else the convoy recedes into the distance in my rearview mirror, leaving me shaking in an impotent rage. Muzamil studies my face for a while and then laughs wistfully, 'You'll get used to it.'

This wasn't an isolated incident. It happened again, unprovoked, on another road trip a couple of weeks later. I realized that it was part of the daily humiliations heaped upon the Kashmiri to break his spirit, but it was impossible to get used to, so accustomed was I to living with my basic rights in my democratic country.

After a few days of travelling in north Kashmir I start feeling a bit frayed and exhausted by the constant talking, engaging and thinking so intensely. In a small village called Arin I go to a house busy preparing for the fortieth day ceremony—prayers and feasting to commemorate the death of eleven family members. They point to the hill in the distance, 'That's where the shelling came from.' I am used to war films of my childhood where shelling meant blackened, cavernous houses without roofs. Here was an example of sophisticated warfare of the nineties: the large house was perfectly intact but for the broken windows, and the family was wiped out.

Over cups of tea in that fast disappearing afternoon I am shown macabre pictures which leave me cold, anaesthetized. It is too much. I cannot comprehend the magnitude of this family's tragedy. Mir, the twin who escaped, keeps up the monologue as if he were showing me photos from a holiday,'And this is my brother, see this is where the shrapnel got him ... this is my mother ... this is ...'The photos are truly ghastly: lacerated lumps of flesh, blackened faces; I find myself wondering about the man photographing, how he continued to take pictures without throwing up—or perhaps he did. One has a little boy lying on the ground with his intestines spilling out. I learned later that he survived. Smiling, he had lifted up his sweater to show me the scar, a nacreous pink ridge that spanned the entire width of his stomach.

It was all a mistake. The security forces on the other side of the hill were after the Hizbul Mujahideen and had overshot their mark. The villagers came out of their houses after a few shells had exploded and that was that. When the government concluded its inquiry into the incident predictably, no one was booked.

While we are talking an older woman walks in holding a child in her arms. We are introduced. She is the woman who has lost her daughter, son-in-law, two grandchildren, her daughter's mother-in-law and a nephew. She holds Jameela, the only survivor, two-and-a-half years old, who witnessed everything. She clings to her grandmother. The woman and I stare into each other's eyes for a long time. I feel my heart heaving inside, yet I am unable to say anything at all. She looks incredibly tired. Then without a word tears begin to roll down her cheek. I reach out and take her hand. We sit there for an age crying softly together. There is nothing else to do. When I am about to leave she takes both my hands and covers them in kisses.

We drive back in silence. The road through the village is narrow. We turn a corner and I see an army truck turning into the road a hundred yards ahead. There isn't space for both of us to pass so I flash my headlights and blow my horn and indicate that I want to turn into the side lane ahead so that he can pass. But instead of slowing down he hurtles towards me and before I can reach the lane he has blocked my path. We are eyeball to eyeball. He expected me to reverse a quarter of a kilometre now. The driver starts blowing his horn and gestures aggressively. A *jawaan* on top leaning against the cab starts shouting, '*Ay bhenchod peechay hutt.*' The others join in and start making obscene gestures.

Something snaps inside of me and before I know it I am washed out of the car in a flood of fury confronting three truckloads of *jawaans*. 'How dare you ... How dare you ...' I roar at the soldier sitting in the cab who looks like he's in charge. We are still shouting at each other, accusing each other, when I feel a hand drop on my shoulder which spins me around and suddenly I've got automatic rifles stuck in my ribs. 'Hello? What's this?' Never having experienced this outside of a Hollywood film I unthinkingly slip into my part. It is so unconscious, so easy, that I hardly know I've got both index fingers straight out like the barrels of a pair of .357 magnums and I'm bellowing at the top of my lungs, 'BACK OFF, BACK OFF, MOTHER F—ERS!'

Miraculously, it works. They stop dead in their tracks and lower their weapons, surprised and then sullen. I flash my press card and Muzamil starts shooting off names of generals he knows. Some guys jump off the truck and pull the others back, some apologize profusely. I whip out my camera and photograph, still taut and trembling with anger, and somewhere, still holding them responsible for the deaths in Arin.

They have many names: the renegades, the friendlies, the Ikhwanis, but most Kashmiris called them dogs because they have reportedly been bought over by the BSF and army and help in the counter-insurgency. They swagger down the main road of Bandipora town in broad daylight, carrying Kalashnikovs, grinning self-confidently. K, travelling with us, had to be hidden. Muzamil on edge and shouting at me on the slightest pretext. We finally had a showdown when I switched the engine off and told him to stop getting so hysterical. Tension between my shoulder blades travelling in a sharp line of pain up my neck. People look at us suspiciously as the white Maruti lurches slowly up potholed tracks leading into villages known to be sympathetic to the renegades. Once or twice we pass patrols of unkempt Ikhwanis, their pouches of ammunition strung about their chests theatrically. K worries about his people, 'I'm leaving tomorrow, but they may come after my family when I'm gone because they've seen me with you.'

On the edge of the Wular lake, in a poor fishing village called Kulhom which smelled rank with weeds and rotting fish, a boy was forced to join the Hizbul Mujahideen and was reportedly shot dead soon after in a joint operation of the army and Ikhwanis. Five months later his younger brother, a schoolboy of just fourteen or fifteen, was allegedly abducted and killed by the same renegades to set an example. The third brother was terrified and went into hiding. I sit there listening to the widow, the mother of these children, recounting the horror of the last few years while her teenaged daughter sobs in the corner. She doesn't have the luxury of mourning for her dead sons. She is forced to beg because there are no earning members left in her family, she herself knows no trade, and the government will not pay compensation to women whose children became militants.

I am sickened by the gratuitous violence and destruction. Outside I notice a newly constructed house which is conspicuous because it stands arrogant and shiny amidst the other fishermen's hovels. It belongs to the Ikhwan commander of this village. I hear stories of other whimsical killings: someone killed because he refused to do salaam to the commander; a mother of eight murdered because she dared to beg them not to loot her neighbour's home. Leaving the widow's house I see a strange tableau being enacted: the commander's wife and mother sit outside their home in the sun cleaning rice like any other village women. I couldn't help but wonder what their lives are like, surrounded as they are by such fear and hate. How is it possible that in the vortex of this terrible and seemingly irrevocable breakdown of relationships and trust, people still continue to live out their lives normally, even mundanely?

I'm getting familiar with this situation: how people use this war to their own advantage. Naive to imagine great principles being lived out. If they were alive at one time, perhaps in the infancy of the *azaadi* movement, they have been successfully snuffed out now by a more powerful and universal force which, ironically, allies the Kashmiri closer to the people of India than they realize: the lust for money and power. In Dachigam, Bandipora, a man is reportedly picked up from his home by uniformed soldiers one night and is never seen again. Four months later I'm sitting in a cold dark room listening intently as the family recount their painstaking efforts to locate him every day. They are turned away routinely from police stations and army encampments. A petty official in the Food Supplies Department, he had been implicated in a corruption case three years ago and then suspended. He fought a lawsuit and won it and was to be reinstated with his dues paid up when he was abducted. Who knows whether he refused someone a cut or whether his innocence implied someone else's guilt?

'If he is guilty of something let him be put on trial and judged publicly. If he is found guilty of some crime let him serve his term in prison. But this? Taking him away like this in the dead of night with me running behind them in the street outside, begging them to let him go, pleading with them to tell me where they were taking him, why they were taking him, what they were going to do with him . . . my son . . . my son . . .' The old woman spoke clearly, forcefully, her parchment eyelids closing when her voice occasionally faltered into breathless sobs.

Another old woman some weeks later in Oonagam, they could be sisters or perhaps even the same, their faces blur in my memory now. But I am hardly to be faulted, the stories being nearly identical but for minor variations. Late on night with the rain pouring down in sheets I negotiate treacherous muddy tracks to the house of Mohd. Iqbal Wani. We had read an innocuous column in the papers about the suicide of this depressive police officer stationed in Qazigund, south Kashmir. Muzamil told me how a few weeks earlier the same man had made the headlines because he had caught and impounded a truck filled with a contraband drug called Descroia.

His hunch proved to be correct. The following morning the large room fills with Wani's weeping relatives, and the story unfolds, coiling about me slowly until I start feeling claustrophobic and want out. The old mother talks of the past, how she was widowed when Mohd. Iqbal was an infant, how she raised him with such love and care. She speaks of his inheriting his father's vast orchards and fields and that if he had wanted he needn't have worked, but he became a police officer because of a childhood dream, and an honest one at that because he was wealthy. And then one day they heard of his big catch, and they grew proud. A week later he surprised them by returning to Oonagam on leave. He looked tense, smoked unusually heavily, spoke about being under tremendous pressure from a local MLA and his colleagues to release the truck and the men he had jailed. He seemed confused, distracted. A few days later when he went to Sopore to visit his sister three men arrived in a blue Maruti looking for him. They said they were sent by the new SP, who wanted Mohd. Iqbal to resume duty immediately. They insisted that his wife and two little daughters accompany them to Sopore. The old widow refused but under pressure took them herself.

When Mohd. Iqbal saw them he allayed his mother's fears. He knew one of the three men; it was his colleague from the Qazigund police station. 'That was the last time I saw him alive because the next morning he was found dead on his desk with a bullet under his left ear.'

A tray of tea is brought in. The old lady insists I eat the boiled egg which is served. I oblige but it gets stuck in my throat. Someone produces a photograph of the officer. He is young and handsome in his uniform. 'Look, look ... does he look like someone who would kill himself?' Her hands shake as she holds the photograph. His young wife, who sat huddled with her two little girls, silent and expressionless all this while, breaks down and weeps.

Suddenly there is a shriek outside and a loud banging on the door. I jump up and am on my feet, tense, expectant (of what?). Someone rushes to the door and speaks harshly in Kashmiri, the wailing and banging increases until the door is flung open and a woman falls into the room. Two men pick her up and take her out. It is Mohd. Iqbal's sister, mad with grief, they explain. I sit down, shaken but before I can recover someone brings the dead man's shoes. 'See, look at the shoes, see how they are polished. Would a depressed man take the trouble of polishing his shoes and going to work early in the morning only to shoot himself half an hour later?' she asks, her eyes searching my face for answers. 'I wonder why I taught him to be honest, upright ... they brought his body here ... he had shaved that morning ... his uniform was pressed. He was always neat, particular ... his uniform was pressed. He was always neat, particular ... None of them came to pay their respects, commiserate; not one police officer.' Her voice cracks and fades into silence. The air grows thick with their collective grief.

'When Mohd. Iqbal wrote, did he write with his left hand or right?' I ask one of the men quietly before I leave.

'Right, of course.'

When we part the old lady showers me with feathery kisses and blessings, as if I would be the one responsible for resurrecting her son; the young widow presses me to her so fiercely that she squeezes tears out of me.

There are so many stories: Hamida, the half widow, so called because her husband was abducted and they have no idea whether he is dead or alive. She spent seven years waiting for him to return. She is still young and beautiful, and would like to remarry, but every time she decides to do so she gets a whiff of a rumour of his being alive, and so resumes another cycle of the familiar, agonizing wait.

In another village young Benazir breaks walnuts for me and tells me about her father. 'Can I show you a photography?' and dashes off before I can answer. 'See, wasn't he handsome?' she asks shyly, 'Everyone said he looked like Rajesh Khanna. He used to ride a motorcycle . . .' The Hizbul Mujahideen reportedly killed him because he was too flashy and drank more than orthodox Islam would permit.

Bizarre stories, unreal, and all the more so because they were commonplace. And all this compounded, made even more surreal by the backdrop of the Wular shining through golden poplars, the Harmukh range glinting silver against a perfect blue sky; soft sunsets, willows, undulating land all in russet tones. Often I would drive by men loading boxes of apples onto horse-drawn carts with large wooden wheels: a scene from another continent in another century; cows and sheep moving slowly through smoky evenings. Men smoking hookahs under enormous chinars. Women carrying samovars on their heads. Some startlingly beautiful faces framed in black burqas.

Back in Srinagar I am grateful for the domestic routine. I am exhausted and they nurse me back to strength by enveloping me in affection: Lucky brings me a flask of tea every morning while I'm still in bed. Some afternoons I tutor Kali, who is panicking before her final exams.

At breakfast time one of Muzamil's *mamas* drops his three-year-old before he heads off to work. She has us all wrapped around her little finger and even I am reduced to crawling on all fours roaring like Sher Khan while she squeals and jumps from lap to lap.

Every evening the three girls crowd around me and ask me questions which range from life in Delhi to the rights of women to Buddhist philosophy. One day I talk about principles of non-violence, or rather the non-viability of violence.

'And *azaadi*? It's a complex issue. I'm no nationalist and frankly it matters little to me whether Kashmir is independent of India or not. However, *azaadi* seems to be a magical word around here, a panacea that will cure poverty, corruption, violence, toothaches—all in an instant. I'm not so sure. For starters, all borders, all territories seem limiting to me, indicate a poverty of the imagination. And yet *azaadi* from oppression, yes, from custodial killings, yes. But all this struggle and death only to replicate the same model—for no alternative has been clearly formulated, and certainly, there seems to be no leader with the required vision to lead you into your promised land—I don't know. For myself, I want freedom from my anger, for example, from fear of all sorts . . .'

They listen intently, stopping me only to clarify a point. 'I don't believe one will find solutions to this mess in any of the choices available today. I think—perhaps a bit foolishly—that the answers lie elsewhere . . .' And then I spoke of the wisdom of Kashmir, which somewhere, because of this war, lies buried: of the Sufis of the past and their rich, highly evolved philosophy. I list their names joyously: Noor-ud-din Wali to the Muslims, Nund Rishi to the Hindus, Sahaj Anand to the Buddhists, the patron saint of Kashmir who predicted this devastation in his verses; Lal Ded to the Hindus and Lalla Arifa to the Muslims, the woman

who danced naked and sang songs of praise that the Shaivites and
the Sufis claimed as their own: Shah Hamdan, Maqdoom Sahab,
Bulbul Shah ...

They, in turn, tell me about their father, who until he died
followed a Sufi of the highest order, Ahad Sahab of Sopore. We
talk animatedly. Soon we are joined by the rest and Behenji tells
me stories about the ageing saint of Sopore, the *Fana al Fana*. Jami
brings a photograph. Muzamil's *khalu* speaks of his own father, a
Pir sahab in Pulwama district who claims a following. Muzamil
tells me about the wise old lady in Vatrad. Suddenly there are a
thousand stories, whirling, swooping, turning about my head like
the pigeons that proliferate in the old quarter of Srinagar.

Long after dinner is done we sit around, *kangris* under our
arched legs to ward off the biting cold. 'Stay. Stay a few more days,
weeks, months, we'll arrange for you to go to all these places. You
can meet Ahad Sahab and Pir Sahab ...' I smile, thinking about all
the pending things in Delhi and my mother waiting for me for
Diwali in Calcutta, but there is no choice to be made. 'Yes, I think
I will.'

That night, curled into my quilt, with one of the girls snoring
softly in the next bed, I find myself awake with delight and hugely
relieved after the hideous monotony of war and death. To have
scratched the minefields and wastelands of Kashmir ever so lightly
and to have been blessed with the promise of such treasures: this
I hadn't dared to expect.

II

The bus struggled up the hill, wheezing and puffing through
apple orchards with deep purple flowers of saffron planted in
rows below. Jami and I were squeezed between a Pathan with a
luxurious red beard, his wives, mothers or daughters in burqas,
and a basket full of his squawking chickens. The road to Charar-
e-Sharif, where the patron saint of Kashmir, Sheikh Noor-ud-
din, lies buried, is less than thirty miles south of Srinagar but we'd

been in the bus for more than three hours before Jami pointed to a hill in the distance.

I remembered so clearly that spring of '94, following the story of the Afghan mercenary, Mast Gul, as he battled with Indian troops from his cover in the shrine. The events that led up to the gutting of the tomb and the town of Charar-e-Sharif are still covered in a haze of mystery, as thick as the black smoke that billowed for days from the charred hillside. Strangely, even after the pitched battle which dragged on endlessly and despite the army cordoning the town, Mast Gul and his cronies managed to escape only to reappear in Pakistan triumphant as crusading knights, and crowing about his escapade. In despair, I paced the drawing room of an old bungalow in a tea plantation in north Bengal listening to the BBC's confused news reports of the army blaming the militants and the Kashmiris blaming the army. It hardly mattered who did it. The point is this: once arms are raised to solve political problems the fall-out is inevitably death, destruction and confusion.

Back in Delhi I took to spending long hours at the library at Teen Murti absorbed in the life of Noor-ud-din and the other saints of Kashmir. What emerged was a rich, finely woven tapestry of the spiritual life of a land now under so much turmoil. I was amazed by the prescience of Noor-ud-din writing in the fourteenth century, his sense of humour and sharp wit, by the wisdom that grew from the fusion of many religious traditions in his heart, which was to become the distinguishing mark of later medieval poet-saints all over India. There were passages of incredible weariness and sadness as if he were witnessing our times:

> Like a king swan I attempted to soar into high heavens
> This world made on owl of me,
> And my wings decayed like fallen leaves,
> The mean shepherd boys encircled me in their grip.
> Precious gold is less than shards of glass

Frightened now, how am I do cross
The sharp-edged narrow bridge
Under which flows
A stream of burning flames?
These grey hairs will fall like rotting leaves.
The warm five fast changes into cold ashes.
The tired king swan is destined to fall into a long sleep.

The bus slowed to a halt in front of a road block near an army camp encircled by barbed wire. A couple of armed sentries climbed on and peered into people's faces, occasionally checking the contents of their bags. They got off a few minutes later and we were on our way again. 'It's gotten much better,' Jami said. 'Earlier we would have been forced to get off the bus while it was searched. Sometimes we'd even have to become *murgas*.'

'What do you mean?'

'Oh sometimes they'd force us at gunpoint to get down on our haunches and walk, clucking about like hens,' he laughed. 'Once there was this doctor we knew who was travelling on a bus which was stopped. They got everyone off, wanting them to move rocks across the road for a bunker that was being built. Now the rest of the bus was filled with poor people, labourers, farmers, who didn't mind that much. But our doctor sahab, poor fellow, was suited and booted and considered it below his dignity to do menial work. Being a reasonable man, he approached the closet *jawaan* and said, 'Look, I'm a doctor I can't do this work.' The soldier looked him up and down and asked sweetly, 'Are you a big doctor or a small one?' Doctor sahab felt it best to puff himself up and reply with utmost solemnity, 'A big one, of course.'

'Then be so kind,' said the soldier, 'as to pick up the big stones and carry them across the road.'

We burst out laughing together, startling the chickens. But we soon withdrew into our individual territories of silence. Ahead, the hill of Charar was alive with hundreds of new tin roofs winking morse codes in the weak sun. The bus trundled to a halt in front of a new township just before the hill of Charar. A shiny new board stood proudly before shiny new houses. The Alamdar Colony, built for those who had lost their homes in the fire, looks more like a Delhi suburb than the small *mohalla* up the hill, behind the *hamaam*, the only part of the original Charar left unscathed. There, the houses are old, as old as the shrine was, perhaps. The wooden beams, the tiny bricks weaving a delicate pattern on the facade, the intricately carved windows, now a faded turquoise, all bear testimony to an older, richer culture.

The shrine itself was a jumble of concrete and tin sheds hastily put together by a government overburdened with guilt. Rusted iron rods stuck out of the roofs as if a hundred skeletal fingers were pointing heavenward, accusingly. Piles of gravel and rubble lay in neglected heaps in the shrine's compound. People milled around aimlessly. The whole place had an air of deadness, lethargy, like the corridors of an ossifying government building. Inside, no, it started at the gates itself: the keepers of the *mazaar*, past masters at the act, aggressively extend their hands for 'donations' before you even enter. At each corner of the glass-enclosed mausoleum sit these faithful *sofis*. I had barely bowed my head in reverence before there was a tap on my shoulder for money, barely touched my forehead to the glass before there was another. Irritated, I asked one of them why there were so many collectors of donations. He led me over the cold cement floor to a corner of the shrine where in a glass aquarium lay the model of the new shrine. It was a melange of vague Islamic architecture, a clumsy coupling of Mughal grandeur and Ottoman opulence. Something designed by an architect from one of the Central Asian republics who was especially commissioned by the Govt. of Kashmir, for whom the perfect proportions of the older shrine were not good enough. But all this fuss was hardly appropriate for a man who sang *Clay my foundation and clay around me, clay is within and clay my destination.*

What is it about our age that even this spirit succumbs to the dead weight of orthodoxy and concrete? The destruction of the shrine by fire is only part of the tragedy of Charar-e-Sharif.

I find a quiet corner and sit and observe. An old man leans his forehead against the mausoleum. A dusty lithograph from another time. He doesn't move at all in the couple of hours that I am there. Women come in groups, mutter prayers, weep softly, kiss the glass with an intensity which is startling. The *sofis* keep up their harassment diligently. One family I watch through a tear in the tin partition. The women prayed feverishly, quickly, while their menfolk played for time, bargaining with the keepers of Charar, *magar hum gareeb hain,* 'we're only poor labourers, saba,' while the fat man persisted in low, insistent tones. Finally the labourer smiled an embarrassed smile, fished into his pocket and slipped a few notes into the hands of the keeper, who then shuffled off to prey on another family. Unlikely that any of this will be paying for bags of cement.

Mullahs have become merchants of mosques, the pandit steals idols from the temple, one among thousands of them may deserve salvation, others are all disciples of Satan, sang Noor-ud-din. He was to found the Order of the Rishis of Kashmir, both Muslim and Hindu, for whom a life of wandering and meditation became the only path to God. The emperor Jehangir visiting this land two centuries later, impressed with the Order, was to write in his memoirs: 'They restrain the tongue of desire and the foot of seeking and eat no flesh. They have no wives, and always plant fruit-bearing trees in the fields so that men may benefit by them, themselves desiring no advantage.' Abul Fazl in the *Ain-i-Akbari* calls them 'The most respectable people of Kashmir ... who although they do not suffer themselves to be fettered by traditions, are doubtless true worshippers of God. They revile not any other sect and ask nothing of anyone ...'

At a *dhaba* outside the shrine's compound Jami and I are joined at the table by a tailor master from Srinagar. He chats amiably between mouthfuls of rice and meat, occasionally push-

ing off the large, inquisitive goat tied near our table. He says he
has come every year for the Urs ever since he was little, and
sometimes he comes just like that, whenever the mood takes him.
He feels at peace here, that's why he comes. Otherwise what's the
need of coming all this way when in and around Srinagar itself
there are so many shrines and *asthaans*?

'Do you know the Sheikh ul Alam's verses?' I ask, struggling
with the meat floating in a pool of oil.

'No. I read the Quran Sharif here.'

'What about other people who come here?'

He grins sheepishly. 'During Urs, the verses are chanted out
loud through the night, but look, mostly people read the Quran
here. The Sufi path is a very difficult one. It was fine for people
in the old days, but now it's different. *Zamaana badal gaya hai.* I
have a wife, children, my work. I have very little time.'

'Are there any Rishis today, I mean, like Sheikh Noor-ud-
din?' I ask

He looks at me, amused, and says nothing.

I can't finish my *lawaaza* and meat curry partly because
there is a man with a hungry look and grubby *pheran* who passes
up and down looking meaningfully at my plate. It is rare to see
poverty in Kashmir. I wrap the roti and meat into a roll and, my
right hand being greasy, I hand it to him with my left. He takes
the food, gives me a sour look, tells me in Kashmiri that you
don't offer food with your left hand and stalks off.

The intermittent showers that started earlier settled into a
light-persistent drizzle by late afternoon, so we decided to head
back to Srinagar. Waiting for the bus to leave, I watched armed
soldiers strut about the square; at the entrance the keepers perched
near large, bilious green safes. A verse of Noor-ud-din's flashed
through my head like a revelation: 'The source fountains shall dry
up, the street gutters shall flow brimful, and then monkeys shall
rule the country.' The bus moved slowly away from the hill of
Noor-ud-din and suddenly I was filled by an inexplicable grief, a

weariness of war and stupidity. Also, a terrible homesickness which
flooded the veins: a longing for warm weather, and peace, yes the
peace of Delhi, of rotis not made of white refined flour, for vegetables, and salad, for a strong espresso and the warmth of friends
and family.

Jami and I watched silently as the world dissolved into a soft
sunset. The hills rolled on until the horizon, gently, like the swells
of a benign ocean or perhaps the slopping shoulders and soft
curving hips of a giant, peaceful race in deep slumber. There are
no harsh edges in this landscape. Kashmir, Afghanistan, Tibet,
Cambodia—all incredible beautiful parts of this earth, once cru-
cibles of magnificent civilizations, sites of great spiritual power,
now reduced to little more than the undifferentiated conflict areas of news reports. The fate of such lands has always struck me as
strange, tragic, underserving.

Somewhere, mid-journey, the bus was boarded by some dark-
skinned labourers who drew attention to themselves and interrupted my preoccupations. A Bihari family like so many I've seen
in the remotest part of the Himalayas, ekeing out a living by hard
labour in extreme conditions: poor, thin, in thin clothing suitable
for Bihari summers, yellow haunted eyes. Even in the children, an
air of hunger and desperation in their faraway look. And then as I
looked around, for the first time, how strange, how alien the bus
seemed, full of well-fed Kashmiris dressed cosily in their *pherans*
and their rhetoric of freedom.

I spend the afternoon at Masood's house photographing his work,
which is impressive, different: large pieces, part painting, part sculp-
ture, which successfully represent the old Sufi spirit. I met him
quite by chance. I had been reading the Kashmiri-American poet
Agha Shahid Ali's book and had talked to Muzamil about it, re-
marking also on the very strong image on the cover. 'Oh, that's by
my friend, Masood sahab. I can take you to meet him. He teaches
at the art college.'

Masood is a quiet man who would happily spend his life sketching in shrines or dreaming away afternoons by the lake. He suffers from lead poisoning, a condition acquired from absent-mindedly drinking from too many jars of paint water instead of the cups of tea left by his wife on his table. She is lovely: warm, intelligent, articulate. I drop formality and call her Bhabi, like Muzamil. We talk late into the evening, sipping delicately scented *kehva*; or rather I listen to stories about the life of an artist who chose to stay back in the valley. 'The first place to be bombed was the old coffee house at Lal Chowk where we all used to hang out,' Masood says laughing sadly, shaking his greying head. 'The old days were marvellous. As young artists we had a wonderful life, surrounded as we were by such beauty. A bunch of us used to take our paints and head off to Nishat on bicycles, or just by the edge of the Dal or some other quiet spot, there were so many . . . and then in the summer artists from all over India would arrive in droves. Often we'd have camps where foreign artists would also participate. It was all very exciting, there was always a flow of ideas back and forth.'

And then it all changed. His voice grew thick as he recounted events of the last decade, the flight of his Pandit friends, for instance, he had so many he wishes they hadn't left. I tell him about the old Pandit woman in the migrant camp in Delhi, of how she would sit in front of her cooler in the middle of that dreadful summer imagining she was back in Kashmir, and that it was cool Kashmiri rain and not the wet machine air that caressed her face.

Masood is one of the few Kashmiri Muslims to acknowledge that the Pandits left the valley out of fear and not because of some twisted government conspiracy. It is almost impossible to convince those who were left in the valley that people don't leave homes that have been theirs for generations simply because someone asks them to. Equally impossible to convince those who have left the valley that their brethren wanted them to join the *azaadi* movement for reasons other than what they cling to: namely, that

the Muslims wanted the Hindus to participate in rallies because
they would be positioned as the forward guard to be wiped out
first by the bullets from the security forces. The old syncretic
Kashmiriyat has been replaced by a new tawdry communalism.
For every Jamait Islami member there is a Panun Kashmiri. Like
jealous lovers they intensely engage with one another, hurl extravagant accusations at each other, are deeply wounded by the
other. In this, they mirror the preoccupations of Hindus and
Muslims throughout the subcontinent.

Masood had an advertising business which was lost in a fire
some years ago. 'No, you don't have to feel sorry. I was deeply
relieved once the shock wore off.' The work had become quite an
ordeal. In the early phase of the militancy, a group forced him to
print their letterheads, a rival outfit did the same, and then both
got furious at him for his seemingly dubious loyalties and threatened him so that he was forced to flee to Delhi. Shortly after that
the police got after him because they thought he was a sympa-
thiser and he spent many days and nights trying to convince them
of his innocence. One day he was allegedly called by the JKLF to
join the organization and to go underground so that he could
help print their propaganda. He had little choice but to slip out of
town until they lost interest. And once when he attended a national artist's camp in Leh someone published a death threat in
the newspapers so that he had to go underground once again
until the pardon he sought was granted. 'You don't know what
we all have been through,' said Bhabi laughing, 'we didn't know
what to expect next, and all we wanted to do was to live peace-
fully.' I saw the gentle humour and deep caring for each other
that kept the anger and bitterness at bay, that kept them sane in a
universe gone mad.

It is nearly dark before we step out to go to Khanqah-i-
Maula, the mosque of Shah Hamdan. We pass Muzamil's house
and I see a familiar figure pacing the road in front. I lean out
of Masood's old fiat and shout, 'Hey hero! Hey Muzamil!'

Muzamil comes to the car, but instead of the smart retort which I expect I see a heavily furrowed brow. 'There's been a bomb blast in Regal Chowk just now and Jami's gone that side on the bike . . .'

My mouth goes dry. 'Shall we go and check?' I ask.

'It's all blocked up. The army is out. We can't. We just have to wait.'

I run into the flat and Behenji and the girls look up expectantly. They are disappointed when they see it is me. I go up and squeeze her shoulder. We look at each other, saying nothing. Masood enters and suggests we carry on anyway and I leave, relieved to be going somewhere, doing something. But later that night it is Jami who opens the door for me, grinning sheepishly, protesting, deflecting my blows and mock anger. And Behenji tells me about the condition of her heart each time one of her seven children steps out of the house.

We drive through unlit, narrow streets. The old houses crowding the edges normally create a pleasant intimacy which is lacking entirely in the fashionable new parts of the city. But today the old quarter seems merely dirty, claustrophobic. The traffic, packed closely together, moves jerkily in fits and starts. The air is tense with the news of the blast. Crowds scurry between cars with lowered heads. Suddenly the army appears out of the darkness, armed and waving cars on aggressively. I'm not so sure that this is the night we should be out sight-seeing. We park on a side street and then join the torrent of cars and people down the narrow alley-way which deposits us at the mosque. In the courtyard we are enveloped by a silence that surprises me; the road with its bustle is still in view. The mosque is just a darker silhouette against the night sky but I am relieved to find that the old, elegant, pagoda-like tiered structure hasn't been replaced by the domes and cupolas of new Kashmiri architecture. A single naked bulb lights the doorway, which is covered by a thick velvet curtain. We step into a

cavernous hall with large crystal chandeliers. The walls are of
carved lacquered wood. Old threadbare carpets line the floor.
On the far side some men sit, heads bowed in prayer. I am
about to step over a low filigreed wall into the hall when there
is a shout freezing my leg in mid-action. 'Please, please, no
women allowed in here.' A greying mullah comes up to us,
apologetic but firm. Bhabhi and he get into a long theological
wrangle in Kashmiri. She has travelled all over the Middle
East, Mecca, Medina, Baghdad, Damascus, Syria. Women are
allowed in mosques in all these places. Why this *zulm*, this
tyranny against women here. Soon she is surrounded by a group
of men; arguing, trying to convince her of the justness of these
laws, but she holds her own remarkably well, deflating their
theories with well-remembered citations from the Quran *and*
hadith. I applaud her silently and step out into the night. I
have had my fill of the shopkeepers of faith. Outside a woman
crouches, lost in prayer under a sign which reads 'Non-Mus-
lims And Women Not Allowed.' Then one of the pious comes
out, hawks noisily and spits into the courtyard. A chuckle es-
capes my lips. He looks at me, puzzled.

I walk to the edge of the compound, to the banks of the
river. The lights from the houses on the opposite side stain the
slow-moving dark water a shimmering gold. Shah Hamdan or
Mir Syed Ali Shah Hamadani, follower of the Naqshbandi *tariq*,
along with 700 Syeds escaping the persecution of Timurlaine,
found their way into the valley in 1372 AD. And thus began
the peaceful conversion of Kashmir to Islam through the mys-
tics of Persia. Sultan Sikandar, the father of Sultan Zain ul
Abidin, was to build this *ziarat* for the saint. But it was a woman,
a mere woman, Bibi Saleha, queen of Sultan Muhammad
Shah, who in the early sixteenth century sold her jewellery to
rebuild the mosque that had been destroyed by the Shias. If
the faithfuls inside knew this bit of history they chose to ignore it.

What happens to a people who forget their history? Or rather, invent their own history? For the politicians and bureaucrats in Delhi and Islamabad the story starts in 1947, each clutching to their version of events ('. . . but the Simla Agreement in 1972 wipes out any promises that Nehru, the idealist, may have made'), and dates like precious jewels. Claimants all. As for the Jamait, they would prefer not to think about the time before Islam; a long Islamic history would link them more closely to Pakistan and other more powerful Islamic nations than India south of the Pir Panjal. Never mind that the first Muslim king was a Tibetan or that Muslim rule, whether it was the Chaks, or the Afghans, was not always beneficial for the people of Kashmir. Never mind that Kashmir has always been closely linked—historically, politically, culturally, spiritually, to India and her people. The Panun Kashmiri dwells on the Lohara dynasty in the early fourteenth century or the follies of the Sikhs and Dogras more recently. They align themselves with the Hindu Right which speaks of an Akhand Bharat and teaching the Muslims a lesson. For the *jawaans* it starts yesterday when they saw their men killed and their blood boiled for revenge. And somewhere, hovering over all of this, the Americans waiting and watching; who knows where they see their historical role?

All of the above is true, all these clamouring histories that compete with each other. But they are islands, self-referential, unconnected to each other. In my brief association with Kashmir I was to learn about the channels and tides which linked these histories through the stories of people. Stories too long and too complex to relate here, stories which hopefully will be told again, elsewhere.

Delhi hasn't seen sun in the last three weeks. Outside the world is drained of colour and mirrors my exhaustion after my trip to Kashmir. I stay indoors, immobile in front of a room heater. Through the window the winter sky is a flat grey which remains unchanged throughout the day. In some remote part of my brain

I recall the depressive of Scandinavian countries and they no longer seem an alien breed. It is the season when one longs to curl up in some giant amniotic sac, to be rocked gently by the nourishing warm fluid. Let the world blow itself up. Let murderers, rapists and thugs profit. It has nothing to do with me. Surely, O Charioteer, the correct response to Kalyug can only be inaction?

Occasionally I scan the papers for news of Kashmir. Another 600-year-old shrine burnt down, and the killings and abductions continue. And then sometimes a longish piece by the ex-governor of Kashmir, the old man with the strange hairstyle: quick recipes for the return of peace.

Something stirs inside me, sluggishly, almost reluctantly.

A friend drops in and shows me the rosy picture painted in a national weekly. It has photos of 'normalcy'—*jawaans* in *shikaras* on the Dal Lake.

I pick up a novel and try and enter another world away from this one but there is a tap on my shoulder which grows more and more insistent. I hear a chuckle whose scorn is impossible to ignore. It is her again, the old nag: Truth, with a capital T. My very own personal one that has shadowed me for aeons, twin sister of Trouble, more burdensome than Sin or even Guilt. She squats atop, 'Now ...' she whispers, 'close your eyes and picture this,' and she dictates. And I, her faithful amanuensis, suddenly have no choice: I must record her story, however imperfect.

(December 1997)

PETER HANLEY

Kashmiri Bundook

When I lived in Kashmir during the fifties and sixties, the ultimate weapon the average Kashmiri might dream of owning would be a bolt-action .303 Lee-Enfield Mk IV, most probably dating from WW II or slightly later.

There were lots of Lee-Enfield rifles scattered about the countryside during the events following the partition of India in 1947. Ammunition of the same vintage was relatively plentiful. There were times when the suspense of waiting to see whether it would go off or not could be almost literally killing—such as a bear charging at what looked like 200 miles an hour, the rifle clicking harmlessly, old Abdullah working the bolt again—click—and again—click—and—again—dud cartridges clattering on to the suddenly not-so-big-seeming rock we crouched upon while the bear got bigger and louder and more and more detailed every hundredth of a second.

When the rifle finally went bang instead of click, it was almost as great a shock as the arrival of the bear itself would have been—for me. But Abdullah was used to this state of affairs, though even his hands were trembling slightly as he glanced back over his shoulder at my undoubtedly cheese-coloured face after the bear had done one-and-a-half somersaults backwards from seemingly two rifles'-length away. That particular bear was a good deal bigger than usual. I still remember the pattern of the cracks in his tongue very well indeed. Abdullah caught my glance of consternation at the weapon in his hands and briskly clacked open the breech. The successfully fired empty cartridge jumped out and tinkled refreshingly on the flat surface of the rock, which quickly reassumed its normal size. We were once again at an altitude of eight feet above bear-level. His thumb went gouging the remaining cartridges down into the half-empty magazine to show me how much room there was for ammunition. 'It holds *eleven* rounds', he said, 'therefore there is no reason for fear.' The heavy fringe on his dashing natural-coloured silk turban swung magnificently about as he nodded emphatically, reaffirming the significance of the magical number in the scheme of human affairs. Eleven is the most important number of all in Kashmir. Many events and decisions and legends are authenticated by its power. The man on whose behalf Abdullah had shot this bear would now in thanksgiving serve sweet tea at the roadside to eleven passers-by personally unknown to him. It was an established method of discreetly offering thanks to such angels as might have helped sort out one's problems from behind the scenes.

Numerous Pathans' astounding expertise with the *Three-naatt* had turned the military eleven-shooter into a legend in its own right, and according to such, two Pathan marksmen could aim at the muzzles of each other's rifles and fire with such precision that the bullets would collide in mid-trajectory. Scientifically speaking, they would have needed much better ammunition to say the very least ... but in everyday reality, most people got by with the *Kashmiri bundook*—a percussion-lock smooth-bored muzzle-loader of frequently uncertain provenance, more predictably unpredictable, and much cheaper and in some ways safer to use on a regular basis. If you were lucky and very very persistent, you could even get a licence for one of those—which meant that you could carry it about in public. But very few felt the need to wear their guns to town. And licensed ammunition, when available, was absurdly expensive.

I was nine when we moved to the piece of land where we would spend the next eleven years, and the first standing orders my younger brother and I received were that wherever we went, and whatever we might be doing, we absolutely had to be within twenty yards of the house before dusk. It would be quite a long time before we actually saw a bear, though we had already heard horrifying stories about what they did to people every summer. And we had met Alia, the *shikari* who had been mauled and then buried alive by a bear years before when a sahib's shoot had gone wrong. During the moonlit nights of high summer, the bears would assemble for dinner parties in the maize fields that spread to the foot of the mountains behind the house.

Bears have highly individual personalities, and most of the time they seemed to prefer dining alone when the corn cobs were worth eating in quantity. Each would leave his or her individual sign of the night's activities. There were the cunning ones who entered the fields at a different point every time they paid a visit, and others (undoubtedly of Very Little Brain) who used the same route so consistently that they created their own distinct private footpaths through the woods and across the close-nibbled pastures. Some would climb heavily over the villagers' pathetic fences of heaped pine branches with a tremendous cracking and snapping of twigs, setting every dog within half a mile frantically barking in the high agitated pitch that warns of dangerous trouble, extra large. Other bears would search out a weak spot among the loosely heaped branches and quietly squeeze their way through, the dogs only waking up when the intruder's scent came drifting into their nostrils. And there were also bears who casually used the villagers' paths and lanes and stiles, but saw no reason to share them with people. They felt very strongly about this—arguing their right of way in simple but compelling terms that any unarmed human being could easily comprehend.

Farming in the mountains of Kashmir is necessarily a defensive activity. In addition to the bears, there are roving bands of monkeys that can devastate a field of maize or a vegetable garden in a matter of minutes. There are hordes of crows with similar intent and wider tastes. If you see enough of your chicks and ducklings carried frantically squeaking into the tree-tops beneath an exultant crow's wings; if you hear often enough the truly hair-raising scream of a hen snatched from her perch by a fox or cat or jackal; if you lose your sheep and dogs to a leopard that sneers from the safety of rocks and thickets that it knows you dare not enter unarmed; or if a bear reduces someone you knew to a basket-load of bloody meat scattered across the mountainside, you're likely to find yourself thinking longingly about guns as a means of protecting your own.

Some years before that afternoon on the rock with Abdullah and his dodgy ammunition, it was clear that we needed a gun if our vegetables and chickens and fruit were to see us through the long and frequently-snowed-in months of winter. My brother and I persistently lobbied our mother to apply for a licence, but actually acquiring one turned out to be a lengthy and convoluted process seemingly designed to discourage the applicant. And she lost interest when informed that all licensed weapons would have to be surrendered to the authorities in the event of war or other comparable emergencies. 'That's ridiculous,' she snorted, 'I'm sure the people who might come shooting at us won't have licences to do so—will they? There wouldn't be any trouble at all if you got them to surrender their guns first!' The official at the receiving end of this had smiled ruefully, tiredly rubbing his eyes. He knew as well as anybody did that unlicensed guns were far more numerous than licensed ones. And he probably knew that we knew about the venison and musk-deer and trout that managed, every so often, to make their way to his table without an official appointment. 'Madam,' he sighed, 'Your theories are no doubt correct, but I am not in a position to act upon them. Perhaps it would be simpler to borrow a gun from a friend or a neighbour willing to help you.' 'Perhaps,' said my mother.

We knew of several people, including a couple of *shikaris*, who had licensed guns. But Resha, our head servant at the time, dismissed the idea of borrowing one with the magnificent contempt that most Kashmiri mountain people have for all things short-sightedly official. He had served my mother and my grandmother before her since he was a boy. 'Memsahib?' he said dramatically, 'If a man's gun is to be taken away from him when he requires it most, is he likely to get a licence for any weapon that is truly of use to him? If it's a Kashmiri gun that you require, I can offer you the choice of fifty good ones within a day. If you want a twelve-bore, or a .303, that too can be arranged. You have only to say what you desire!'

'Er, well', said my mother, slightly overwhelmed by the prospect of such quantities of artillery laid suddenly at her feet, 'what we need is something that'll deal with these wretched crows and foxes, and the monkeys as well whenever they come along. Broca's in Srinagar quoted a frightful price for, umm, twelve-bore cartridges, and I'm not sure that getting a .303 is a good idea just yet. So we'd better think about these Kashmiri guns you were talking about.'

Kashmiri guns were indeed plentiful, and we thought about them for a long time. We thought about twelve-bores and .303s as well when we were offered the chance to do so, and soon we knew of lots of guns to think about.

The *Kashmiri bundooks* of those days came into being from a variety of sources. They ranged from the crude confections of a village blacksmith to the refined and elegant products of 'the hills', meaning Riasi, Rajouri and the southern parts of the Valley. Properly known as *Küshur-bundük* wherever Kashmiri is spoken, muzzle-loaders were widely available because they were easy to manufacture. It's a long journey from the crude 'hande-gonne' of the fifteenth century to the outstanding craftsmanship of the muzzle-loading target rifles wielded by today's American black-powder enthusiasts—but the muzzle-loader consists essentially of a strong metal tube plugged at one end and provided with some means of igniting the gunpowder with which it is charged. A small hole drilled at an angle through the base-plug allows access to whatever it is that does the igniting. This may be a smouldering piece of string, as in the match-lock, a shower of sparks in the case of a flint-lock, or a spurt of flame from a percussion-cap. The muzzle-loader is a reasonably eco-friendly weapon, and the materials required to produce gunpowder are widely available.

The first muzzle-loader I had an opportunity to use was a Kashmiri classic made from the steering column of a pre-war Ford. The barrel was thirty-nine inches long, and wonderfully accurate when loaded with ball. This particular weapon was held in high esteem because its owner had felled a maize-guzzling bear on the far side of the river flowing past his house. Guns quickly acquire individual reputations and personalities in those mountains, and going to see this one was almost like visiting a person. We sat upstairs on embroidered rugs in a balcony overlooking the river bank, drinking *kahwa* and enjoying the flaky *bakirkhanis* we dipped in it while chatting about this and that. Our host could guess why we were there, but owning a gun was a luxury allowed to enter the conversation at its own unhurried pace. So, after we had burped emphatically to indicate our appreciation and the state of satiety arrived at, the tea things were cleared away, the hookah was brought forth, and we sat contented in rhythmically bubbling tranquillity when Resha at last allowed his eyes to stray over the fields across the river. It was early spring and the lace-thin layer of silvery wet snow that remained upon them would soon be gone. He talked of ploughing, and crops, and pests, and at last it was possible to ask about the bear and the gun that had got it.

'Ah, yes, that . . .' said our host as though remembering something insignificant but not quite forgotten. 'Yes, it was sitting under the larger of the two walnut trees halfway up the hill there, eating as though at a wedding.' He indicated a spot perhaps 150 yards away across the river. 'I was sitting where you are now, drinking tea late in the evening. The full moon was rising, and I could see this bear clearly against the grey bark of the tree, eating and eating without any other thought in the world . . . I remarked that it was nearly as bad as having a brother-in-law who does no work; and my wife placed the gun before me. I rested it on the railing there, aiming very carefully. And, by the grace of God, I was pleasantly surprised, for that bear's time had come . . . Would you like to see the gun?' It was a strange-looking weapon, somehow reminiscent of an ant-eater. The gunsmithing was rough and ready, but obviously done by a man who knew his stuff, and the hammer had been shaped entirely by free-hand forging, so well done that it needed no further filing into shape. The stock was a strange-looking affair fitted by one of the local blacksmiths. The owner was flattered but understanding of the young sahib's desire to borrow it for a while, and I shortly discovered that muzzle-loaders can be quirksome in strangely consistent ways. This gun would always fire reliably during target practice, but one could never be entirely sure of it in the field. I soon lost count of the occasions when whoever was using it would draw a bead on quarry patiently stalked, only to have the hammer click harm-lessly. A crow would immediately realize that something was up, taking off to circle overhead before flapping away to inform the world, cawing derisively at the top of its voice.

I well remember the day Resha's son managed to crawl within yards of a particularly nasty wild cat that had terrorized our chickens almost every night during the winter. The gun was freshly loaded, and the cat sat licking a hen's blood and feathers off its paws in a sunny bower beneath the newly planted hedge. My mother, my brother and I, Resha, and a couple of lesser servants watched in admiration as Walia inched his way across the field using every possible bit of cover, angling

cautiously and with infinite patience into a down-wind position, freezing into total stillness every time the cat paused to
briefly scan its surroundings. There was a strong breeze blowing, rustling the hedge. When he was so close that it was impossible to miss with a charge of buckshot, Walia softly thumbed
back the hammer and took aim. Long moments passed. The
tension of waiting for him to pull the trigger became unbear-
able. And then, crisp on the wind came the click of the hammer. The cat glanced up for a moment and casually continued
locking its paws. With careful slow movements Walia cocked
the hammer and aimed again. The world froze into stillness.
The tension mounted. The hammer clicked. The cat paused
and looked about for a few seconds, more carefully this time,
then returned to its task. Walia again pulled back the hammer,
unhurriedly returning to his aim. We stopped breathing. We
waited. The hammer clicked. The cat looked up with twitching ears, turning its head from side to side, suspicious now, but
still relaxed. Snugly sheltered from the sharp spring breeze
and full of a hefty chicken lunch, it didn't want to move unless
it had to. Walia lay motionless and somehow invisible while
the cat scanned its surroundings with alert eyes and ears for
many long seconds. The breeze lifted a few fluffy feathers into
the air. The cat hooked at them playfully with its claws and
then went back to the job in hand. Walia once again prepared
to shoot, and again we waited. It was all a little bit easier the
fourth time around—and the hammer clicked harmlessly. By
now the cat's sixth sense was definitely functioning. It could
feel that something was wrong. It rose to its feet and stepped
from beneath the hedge. Suddenly it saw Walia clearly, whisked
its tail, and smoothly vanished into the woods. Walia stood up
and cocked the gun again. Aiming at a tree, he pulled the
trigger. The gun fired perfectly. He laughed.

   A few days later Mullah Doi, a distant neighbour, dropped
in for tea one afternoon. He had heard about the cat hunt. '*Meem-*

sahib,' he finally said, gouging the sludge of breadcrumbs and sugar from the bottom of his cup and slurping it loudly off his finger to indicate pleasure, 'I would say the Kashmiri gun is a trial that can be avoided! Needless are the uncertainties that attend its use! Infinitely better is the gun that uses cartridges! Haji Gul has such a one—licensed, and truly a gun to be seen! Go! See with your own eyes! And the village may be rid of this cat!' He stroked his magnificent beard, murmuring thanks to God for the tea.

It was indeed a gun to be seen. Haji Gul was a Bakkarwal—a member of the nomadic goat-herding tribes impatient with the fripperies of civilization since time immemorial. They lived in tents and followed the seasons. Their goats flowed over the mountainsides in flocks of several thousand at a time, and the physical barriers of political boundaries were an irksome mystery to them. The Bakkarwals in turn were an irksome puzzle to bureaucracy, and attempts were under way to make them settle down. Haji Gul had succumbed, but his wife clearly had not. She stood, arms akimbo, as we approached her camp. As soon as the snow had cleared, she had moved the household out under the trees again. 'Peace be upon you!' she said, 'And what brings you here? Where are you going?'

'We seek a gun', said my mother, 'we heard that you have one.'

'Yes! There is a gun. There is a licence as well! Is this the only place to seek a gun?'

'They seek to buy one', put in Khan, then a junior servant, but a wiser diplomatic choice for this mission. His people were semi-nomadic, and they had many words in common.

'Ah! The Haji is not here, the gun I will show you—but I need it myself!' She strode to the heaped-up saddle-bags and tugged an elaborately embroidered gun-case from among them. She was tall and rangy like most Bakkarwal women, and slipped the gun from its cover with practised hands. There were silver coins nailed to its stock, a tassel of beads and cowrie-shells swinging from the fore-piece. She dropped open the breech and then thrust the gun at my mother with both hands. 'It's empty. Examine it, and then shoot if you will!'

My mother had not yet learnt to shoot, and gestured it into my hands.

The gun was plainly finished, but seemingly well made until I snapped the breech. Instead of locking up tightly, the barrel wiggled loosely in my hand. I shuddered at the thought of firing it, and regretfully handed it back.

Mrs Gul looked at me contemptuously. 'You are afraid to fire this gun! But I, I use it whenever I need! This gun is not for people such as you. Enquire among your cities. Go in peace— and may you find what you seek!'

We had enquired among our cities. And we had found what no sensible person would seek. The Srinagar museum has a fascinating and surprising collection of firearms. Many of them originally belonged to the Maharaja and include fine examples of English and French gunsmithing, some dating back to the eighteenth century. Most of the royal guns are beautifully carved and chiselled all over and embellished with gold inlay by the original makers. There were cumbersome nineteenth century English revolvers and dainty little percussion-lock pistols. There were flint-lock fowling pieces, and revolving rifles, and half a dozen different kinds of early European breech-loaders. And there was a very rare example of an English breech-loader developed before cartridges were invented. The breech-block was raised and lowered on a quick-screw by cranking the trigger-guard, gunpowder and shot being poured into the gun in reverse order. Guns like this were a failure because they soon sprang a leak, but the royal example was exquisitely made, and of very high value to a knowledgeable collector.

There were guns of all kinds, many of them rare and valuable and quite irreplaceable. And all of them, every single one, had a wide V-shaped slot filed deeply into the barrel, cutting it halfway through. This is what the law requires of any gun not actually licensed for use. No matter that the gun may be so old it cannot be used even if licensed. No matter that antiques are not meant to be treated like this. No matter that the official vandalism could have been perpetrated on the concealed part of the gun's barrel in order to preserve appearance. No matter at all, so long as bureaucracy could be seen to function. One day, perhaps, the dome of the Taj Mahal will bear chiselled letters twenty feet high instructing people not to urinate against the walls. For the moment, the antiques locked up in the museum were ultra-safe, and Mrs Gul lived with the licensed possibility of blowing her own head off sometime in front of a startled leopard.

Meanwhile the .303s remained un-hacked among the safer reaches of the mountains, the bears had something to think about, and the days of the acclaimedly infallible Kalashnikov lay far in the future.

It's a long time since the last time I was in Kashmir. Abdullah moved on to happier hunting grounds many years ago, and by now Resha has probably followed him. In a nostalgic mood the other day, I bought some modern Kashmiri music. The Sufic exhortations to peace and gentleness were still a recurring theme: 'Put your resentments aside, and step out with the others! Brahma has given you no shortage of brothers.'

But times have changed. *Kalashankoff* is another of the new Kashmiri pop songs:

Nüy wala, me gham t' Khof,
Me'iy wan'ha' Kalashankoff!
Aaz ma'ni' war' as os,
Me'iy wan'ha' Kalashankoff!
(Don't talk to me of regret and fear,
Say to me, 'Kalashnikov!'
Today my turn has come at last,
Say to me, 'Kalashnikov!')

The song has a thumpingly cheerful rhythm firmly rooted in the *Chakri* folk tradition. The subtleties of each verse are numerous and witty, and difficult to translate with my very rusty Kashmiri. If the words are to be taken at face value, unreliable guns, at any rate, are now a thing of the past. And I wonder about the future.

(May 1996)

LATHA ANANTHARAMAN

In Dependence

They dribble me back and forth at the Department of Social Welfare on Canning Lane, between a joint director and a woman in room 19 who is addressed only as 'Medam'. It is the load-shedding 'hour' and the sole signs of sentient life in these buildings are pigeons mating on the windowsills and the insistent *tok tok tok* of a coppersmith. I am here to get official permission to visit a widows' home. Anand Khullar, the joint director, has asked for my file to be processed urgently. Medam looks at the single-paragraph letter of mine as if it is written in Greek, her jaw dropped in perpetual astonishment that, when there is 'no light', I should ask for a file to be found. The Special Officer is not here. At four, in about half an hour, the light will come, and then perhaps the file can be found. I am not asking for it to be found, I explain, I have brought a duplicate letter in the full expectation that my file is never to be found again, because the director, who has been unavailable for the ten days since I wrote that letter, has apparently taken the file with him. 'Is Mr Khullar in his seat?' No, not at the moment. 'Well then where can you get the permission from?' If the letter is prepared, I suggest, Mr Khullar is ready to sign it. He has only stepped out briefly. 'What home is this?' she asks, flipping languidly through a green catalogue of the various schemes of the DSW. I give her the name of the home, its location, the name of its superintendent, but she refuses to credit my fantasy.

I know it exists.

The women in white

I see a pale, slight figure carrying water cans, walking toward a boys' school. When I tell her I want to talk to some of the women who have come from Bangladesh, she takes me in. The widows' home leads off an unmarked door to the right of the school. My first sight is of a dark corridor leading into a courtyard, in which young and old women are washing pots and clothes and bathing children. *Ki?* says one, as she sees a stranger in the hall. I wish to speak to some of the Bengali women who came here originally, I say. There is a muted exchange in Bengali, and a man in loose pyjamas appears in one of the doorways. Would you like to sit inside? he asks in English. I am graciously received, apologies are made for the awkward arrangements of the room, which is cramped but clean. Some light filters in from a dusty ventilator set high in the wall. A child peeps at me from behind a curtain and disappears. The man in front of me, Chandu Sarkar, asks me what paper I work for, and almost immediately launches into an explanation.

The 125 Bengali families in the home consist of a group of widows and their children who left Bangladesh in 1964. There are also about 165 Punjabi families. Some are living in quarters, and about thirty-five families are living in these barracks, each portion divided and shared by two families, and then subdivided with woven *chattais* and sheets to provide some privacy. 'We are not refugees,' says Sarkar. 'We have yellow cards. The Government of India brought us out of Bangladesh. In 1964 to Mana Camp and in 1967 to this place. Since then we have not got permanent settlement. We have lived in these barracks for almost thirty years.'

His tone carries no resentment. 'The government has done many things for us. They have given us food, education, some shelter, whether it is less or more. If they want to give me a *katori* of rice I cannot say I will only eat *pulao*. Our demand is only to get [permanent] shelter. Then we can take care of ourselves. These are like huts, there is no privacy, no security. I will show you this place, and you can talk to the women.'

Outside in the courtyard, the first woman we approach shakes her head in exasperation, puts her hands to her ears, and walks off to hang up her washing. But others are eager to have their say. Alomati Mandal is small and brisk and her eyes hold mine with intensity. She takes me to her dim room and seats me on a bare wooden cot. 'I was twenty-two, twenty-four when I came. I have a son and a daughter. We came from Dhaka. Indira Gandhi told us to come. She said we will do everything for you. Just come. But they haven't done anything.'

I am suddenly aware that the room is now full of men, and there is another woman in white looking curiously over their shoulders at me. They apparently take me for an investigative reporter and during the conversation that follows my attempted clarifications have no effect. Without preamble one of them, who introduces himself later as Bimal, begins to state their grievances. 'There are thirty-five families living in the barracks. All together we are 285 families, Punjabi and Bengali. They told us we would all get houses. Even those who came on their own and built *jhuggis* wherever they liked, they have got settled, but we, who were brought by the government, after all these years we have no houses. In the beginning we were living along with the mentally retarded. Write all this . . . which paper are you from? Many reporters have come. Write it strongly.'

Alomati urges me to do something about their problems, but she is interrupted by Sudhir, a man with long black locks who has settled down cross-legged and lit a cigarette. 'The women will mix Bengali and Hindi, how will you understand them?' I assure him I will manage, but he and Bimal have captured the stage just now. 'The Congress government has promised us again and again we will give you houses, but till today they have done nothing. Even the heads of the department of social welfare, they do not take action. They show that it is done, but no one here has received anything. Fifty boys have done their ITI, many have done their technical education, but no one has got work through the government. Our mothers say we were better off in Bangladesh.'

Amodini Madhu, the woman standing behind them all, says, 'We had land, we had homes. Indira Gandhi said come in just your *dhotis*.'

Sudhir brings us back to the matter at hand: 'There are sixty-six quarters. Instead of one quarter per family, they were giving two or three to some of the families. Now only ten families remain there. Why not give us at least the remaining quarters?'

Are those quarters locked or are outsiders living there? 'Three or four are locked. Then some people have put their relatives there. Those who are nearby find out which ones are empty and then they take over.'

'I'll explain clearly what they have done,' says Bimal. 'Congress made themselves a vote bank. There are 2000 votes here. When these women had to vote they tied ropes.' He gestures to show ropes along the queues to the ballot box. 'They said put the stamp on the Hand. We will give you enough to eat and drink and a place to sleep.'

Alomati says, 'The government is just waiting for us to die. Many have died. Then what will happen? We want houses registered in our names. Tell them this.'

Sudhir breaks in, 'All those who are living in Defence Colony are refugees. They all have allotments. If you can give it to them, why not to us? All of those who came from Pakistan have got houses.'

Boren Roy, who had also co me here as a small child, says, 'All the Kashmir refugees who came recently, Madan Lal Khurana settled them in Delhi, when he was MP just before these elections.'

Discussions are still pending with the Ministry of Welfare about the 'forty square yards' that were offered in Kale Khan. The superintendent declined to speak to the Minister for Welfare for them, says Chandu Sarkar, and told them they should address him directly.

They pull documents out of their trunks to show me. Alomati shows me her 'yellow card', and Amodini brings a certificate from Rehabilitation Services. These women constitute a 'permanent liability', according to a note later shown to me at Rehabilitation Services. Their dependent children are entitled to be taken care of till the girls are married and the boys turn eighteen, but the government's responsibility to the widows continues till their death.

Amodini leads me in and out of the maze the partitions have made. 'There is only one way out of here if there is an emergency. We have our cylinders and *chulas* just next to our beds. Can married couples live in such a place? The widows get cooked food, one *katori* of rice, one *katori* of *dal,* one *katori* of *sabji* in the morning and the same in the evening. Now they give us both meals together. Can we fill our stomachs on that? There used to be bread in the morning but they stopped that. There is milk on fifteen days of the month and no milk on the other days. Sometimes they give us saris like this.' She rubs the end of her sari between her fingers.

'We worked in the [training and rehabilitation] centres, cutting and stitching. We got a little money, from which they cut something. We could not fill our children's stomachs on that. I worked in houses, washing vessels in the morning, rushing to the centre, then washing more vessels. We swept and mopped. Like that we used to get 200–250 rupees.'

'They worked in Punjabi houses,' says Seema Sen, one of the younger women who has been translating the Bengali-Hindi combination into plain Hindi for me. 'Then their sons grew up and could earn money to take care of the mothers. Now they don't work in people's houses.' She takes me to her mother-in-law, Sudharani, a squat, silent woman who is chopping up onions and garlic by the muted sunlight coming through the window. At first she only nods to confirm what Seema and Amodini are telling me, never raising her eyes from her work. 'She came with her small boy. She lived in the village of Khulna, she had a house, land.' Sudharani talks reluctantly, her eyes still lowered. 'The Mussalmans troubled us. They beat us. The government brought us here in a steam launch. I brought my six-month-old boy. He was so sick. I got an allowance of forty rupees a month. With that I fed him and bought his medicines. We have seen a great deal of sorrow. I have not got fat from eating. I worked in houses. In the centre we made uniforms, badges, did mirror work.'

Seema says, 'When they gave the money for stitching they would deduct some. The women had just come from Bangladesh. What did they know about the money? They just took what they got.'

Amodini says, 'In a month maybe we got fifteen or twenty-five rupees at the centre.'

Another widow walks in, the one who had first shown me into the barracks. Her name is Saraswati Ghosh. The others ask her to talk to me. 'What should I say?' She asks with a weary smile. Amodini points her toward the tape recorder. 'Say I want quarters, I want quarters, behenji, I want quarters. That's all.' They all laugh.

'We have been here thirty years,' says Saraswati. 'We left our lands in Borishal village. My daughter was one-and-a-half then. She still lives here. I had a boy. When he was fifteen he died'.

Amodini breaks in, 'They did not give him the right medicines. There is only a *sarkari* doctor here, and when they took the boy to hospital he died.'

'After that I just don't talk much any more,' says Saraswati, and we all fall silent. But as I am leaving the barracks she comes close to me. 'Can I tell you something? I have just been washing vessels in a house. We want our own homes. We are all close to death, but let us have some peace in our hearts. Let us see our children settled.'

The widows' home is located in Kasturba Niketan, along with several others of the Department of Social Welfare's eighty-one schemes for the betterment of the poor, the orphaned and the widowed. To get to it I go behind the Central Market at Lajpat Nagar, past pastry boutique and ornate *kothis,* where a narrow gate opens on to a dirt road. A sign names a home for the mentally handicapped. The track winds past a garbage dump and an autorickshaw lying on its side, and I am on an open ground. The scattered buildings are painted in PWD grey and yellow. Among them are the well-kept staff quarters, each fronted by a small garden. Twenty-three staff members keep this concern going. Since the scheme began, how many government servants, I wonder, have retired from these jobs?

The Punjabi families were brought to Kasturba Niketan in 1950 and the Bengali families in 1967, in what was a 'temporary arrangement' until the families could be settled in their own homes. In 1974, the responsibility of caring for them until settlement passed from the Ministry of Welfare to Rehabilitation Services. These matters are explained in the offices I visit, but they raise more questions than they resolve. What kind of temporary arrangement runs nearly five decades? What happens when a refugee meets the government machinery? And the people behind the numbers—how do they live in this limbo enforced on the one side by bureaucratic stasis and on the other by their own inaction, fed by the expectation that something will be done for them?

Bitterness and jamuns

The quarters are one-room tenements little better than the barracks. A few have been extended, clumsily or brazenly. As I walk in the narrow, muddy lanes, which are steaming in the heat,

I glimpse rooms completely filled with people. The power has gone off, and young children are playing cards or chasing each other. Later, in the Rehabilitation Services office, Savita explains that some of the residents in the quarters sublet and some of them extend the structures, all illegally, but the DSW has no authority to stop them, as the land still belongs to the central government. She says, 'They are living very well, better than us.'

Here, among the Punjabi families, the bitterness seems harder than in the barracks. Harbans Kaur, straight-backed and stern, says she left Pakistan at the time of the Partition, while she was still in her early teens. She came with her parents and daughter. Harbans speaks to me in monosyllables and, after seeing that I have got a glass of water, abruptly goes inside. Her young grandsons are more expansive, but their point is brief. She has been here nearly fifty years, and she has not been permanently settled. Her accommodation here is not registered in her name. 'We are supposed to get registered homes. In the ... Indira Gandhi Complex.' (They are not quite sure of the name.) Were they brought here by the government? A man passing by in the lane stops to answer, as the boys have no idea. 'Yes, it was in Nehru's time. The widows were brought here.'

Can I talk to other women? They direct me to the end of the lane, where I can see women sitting on *charpoys* under a *jamun* tree. I approach and ask if I may talk to the two elderly ones. The younger women tell them, 'She wants to talk to you about the Partition!' One of them energetically shakes her head and throws up her hands. 'If I talk to you I'll be sick in the night.' A girl signals to me not to bother that one and to come to the other side.

The younger women make room for me to sit down, but they all continue to point out the futility of my visit. 'What is the use of talking about it?' 'You can see how we live. There is one tap provided by the government. The rest is all privately done.' She waves her hand at the black PVC water tanks on the roofs of the quarters. 'People like you come to rake up our sorrows.' And indeed, as I look toward one of the widows, I see her eyes are wet and pink. 'These women have come from Dulband, Lahore, Rawalpindi, Layalpore.' A man has stopped near me and adds, 'They were all widows and brought small children with them. While the children were small there was an allowance, and some food. When the children turned eighteen all that was stopped. The women worked in the training centres, cutting and stitching and also embroidering.'

There is some confusion about pensions. One woman says nobody gets one, but the man says, 'You don't know, some are getting, some are not getting. What is the use of talking?' With this he goes on his way.

Clearly my already thin welcome has worn out. I thank them and get up to leave. Then *she* calls me, the one who had refused to talk in the beginning. Her name is Janaki. 'Come here, sit with me. What do you want to know?' Her voice is now calm, gentle. 'I came here when I was very young. I was a refugee. My entire family, my husband, all the in-laws . . . all gone. I just came away with my little daughter and the clothes I was wearing. The Mussalmans beat us out of Pakistan. They hit me here.' She pushes away the silver hair to show me a spot above her left ear. 'And here, on the back, on the shoulder.' Her voice trails into silence. My eyes wander to the tattooed dots on her chin and cheekbones. The others have forgotten about us in their chatter and the girls are gathering *jamuns*.

After long minutes, she asks me, 'What else? Will you have some *chai*, some water? *Jamun?* Have you had your food?' I ask how she had been brought here. 'I was in so many places. I don't know the names . . . There was a boy. I had a boy, he was born in Lahore as we were coming. But we were in lorries . . . there was no milk for him. He lived fifteen days and then he died . . . I will go mad thinking about it. *Hum dukhi hain.* It has been so long.

'Here in the quarters it is burning when the sun is hot. We cannot sit inside. Then in the rain the water pours inside, and things start breaking. One boy was hit on the head when some bricks fell. We need proper homes. At least this place should be ours, registered in our names. All the parties make the same promises. We are ready to serve this nation, but our concerns should be addressed. There are many votes here, all the women, their children and even grandchildren. Do that much for us. Then we can have some peace in our minds before we die. Jagmohan said recently that he would get us settled. He may do it.' She looks at me intently, 'Will you write to Jagmohan?'

Putting up

I recall all this while Medam flips through her green book. Among the eighty-one schemes are a Poor House and the Home for Able Disabled and Diseased Female Beggars. The infrastructure seems out of all proportion to the task, and has perhaps forgotten the task. Meanwhile, I begin to understand my own quest in its context. If some widows have been waiting nearly fifty years for homes, why shouldn't I wait ten days for permission to visit them?

Despite my experiences with sundry offices of circumlocution, I tense hopefully at a slight straightening of Medam's spine, but she is only reaching for a cardboard to flap up a breeze with.

'If there were light, something could be done.' Then, after a few more flips through the book and flaps with the cardboard, 'If Shekhar were here ...'

Two more servants of the Indian people drift in. They too look at my letter with pained surprise. What home is this? What department does it come under? How can we give permission? Medam has a brainwave: 'This should go to Jamnagar House! Mrs Savita should give permission.' They all wait for me to leave. But Mrs Savita sent me here, I tell them, and your director has told me that in his absence Mr Khullar will give me the permission letter. Sighs of momentary defeat. Then one of the men

concedes that permission can be granted at this office, since the
director has no objection.

But this is only the beginning of a new discussion among
See No File, Hear No File and Put Up No File. It promises to
carry on till the magical hour of five. Finally, Shekhar, Welfare
Officer, Mumble Division, calls me to his desk.'Please write briefly',
taking out a sheaf of typing paper,'what eggjectly is your purpose.'
I have done just that in the typed letter he is fanning himself with.
'This?' He scrutinizes it as if seeing it for the first time. 'Is the
director here?' he asks the other man. No.'Well then', tossing his
pen on the table,'nothing can be done.' Mr Khullar, I say evenly,
has said that since the director will not return till Monday, he
himself will sign the letter. Sighs. 'See medam, I think you are
dealing with government department for fust time. This cannot
be done in just ten minutes.'

He's mistaken. It's not my first time. If I cross my eyes a bit I
can picture myself back in the Directorate of Advertising and
Visual Publicity, or the Foreigners Registration Office; the Godrej
typewriters and cabinets are the same, as are the files tied up in
white string, and my rump remembers well the plastic cane weave
on those chairs. Out loud I say only, 'It has been ten days.'

'I will put up the file,' he offers. 'And you will get the letter on
Monday morning.' I am familiar with this trick. Monday is sure to
be a little-known restricted holiday, or the first day of his annual
leave, from which he will return in October. But I wait stonily for
him to finish writing a two-line instruction, stopping at every
stroke to heave a sigh of fatigue and shake his head in despair. It
takes him about ten minutes.'Medam, we have been giving permission for so many journalists all these years. We have never refused
anyone.' No, I'm sure you haven't. It's easier waiting for us to die.

On Monday morning, however, the scene at the DSW is
completely different. The open ground in front of the offices is
carpeted with the aged, come to collect pensions and benefits.
Preserving my clothes from the *beedis* the women are smoking, I

press past the crowd to room 19. Medam smiles up at me. 'Your letter is ready. And your file is here.' I am floored. She waves me into the Special Officer's room. Here Ms Prabha Mathur's presence is clearly the figure in front of the ciphers. (Or maybe I presumed too much from the Friday afternoon lethargy last week?) She is crisp, clear and encouraging, and tells me not to worry about the wording of the permission letter, which prohibits photography.

My official visit to Kasturba Niketan is confined to the superintendent's office. Mrs Chawla tells me what has been provided to the inmates by way of shelter, training, clothing, rations, health care and children's education. Some inmates receive a cash dole of Rs 50 a month, and some receive the food and other benefits. Much of what she says is confirmed by the three unnamed inmates who have been brought in to talk to me, till Mrs Chawla says, 'The government has got jobs for many of the children also.' To which the response is an unequivocal 'Na!' She tries to rephrase the claim in order to get their agreement, but the women are firm on that point. I am taken aback when she says, in their hearing, 'When they die their cremation also will be taken care of.' At the end of the visit she summarizes for me their main concern. 'On their behalf I can tell you this. What they require is their own homes, where they can live independently. Just as all of us aspire to live in our own homes, they have the same desire.'

'Just a place of our own', an old woman in white says, 'a place for us to lay our heads.'

Mrs Savita back at Rehabilitation Services emphasizes that the land is available. A meeting was held on the subject of settlement in August 1995, and earlier a space of forty square yards was promised, but no decision was taken. Does it look like the present administration will settle them? 'The government should take an early decision,' she says. 'How long can these people wait?'

Just a little longer, and death may resolve the questions.

(August/September 1996)

RUCHIR JOSHI

The Death of a Tall Man

The wake

I spent the evening of 23rd April 1992 drinking with two friends of mine in Olympia Bar, on Park Street.

All three of us had something to do with the cinema. The oldest of us had been involved in Calcutta's film society movement since 1960, the year I was born. The other, also older than me, was a well-known film critic. My own concern with serious films—as a documentary filmmaker—went back a paltry ten years at the time and so, as juniors do, I mostly listened.

Ignoring the rats scurrying around our feet, we drank rum and soda and argued about a short film we had just been to see. As the drinking progressed, the film got left behind and the conversation turned to memories and gossip. Inevitably we came around to the two figures who have towered over contemporary Bengali cinema—Satyajit Ray, and Ritwik Ghatak—a director far less known than Ray but regarded by many as the greater of the two. Ghatak had died sixteen years before, in 1976. Ray, as we all knew, was at that moment in hospital, lying on what was probably his deathbed.

Someone mentioned the Oscar for Lifetime Achievement

that Ray had received in his hospital room a few days ago.

'All his life he wanted an Oscar. Those pirates in Hollywood finally rush here with their bloody video camera only when they realize he is dying. Had he been all there, he might well have refused. I mean, look at the French. They gave him the Legion d'Honneur when? 1985? Why should Satyajit Ray have to wait for the Academy's Lifetime Achievement award till after it has been given to every second rate American director?'

'I don't think he would have refused. Ritwik might have, but not our Raybabu.'

'If he'd been alive, Ritwik would have laughed.'

'Yes. "Manik why are they giving you the Oscar for *Charulata* now? You made the film in '64!"'

'"Manik, these Hollywood people are even stingier than you. They sent it by such a slow boat, it took twenty-eight years! Look, even your son has grown up since you last made a decent film!"'

'Oh Ritwik could be nasty.'

'Very nasty . . . listen, did I ever tell you this one? I shouldn't really.'

The film society man launched into a story: 'This is from the early sixties. By then, Ritwik had made three great films one after the other, but no one had noticed. While Ray was already being compared to Kurosawa and Bergman by foreign critics.'

'So . . . one Sunday morning, Gariahat Market sees a strange sight. Ritwik Ghatak shopping for vegetables. Why? Because, if his wife had sent him to market, it meant that she had given him money. And giving him money normally meant Ritwik heading straight to the country liquor shop.' A waiter stopped next to our table, caught by the story.

'But today, here is Ritwikbabu, a shopping basket in one hand, actually buying vegetables. Ritwikbabu doesn't look happy and the reason for his unhappiness is held in the crook of his other arm. Ritwik has been sent to market not only with money but also with a sweet little baby girl—his niece's daughter. Why? Because Mrs Ghatak knows that whatever Ritwik may do for a drink, he would never be able to show his face at the booze shop with a baby. Checkmate.' My friend took a sadistic swig of rum.

'So, the shopping basket is filling up, almost by itself. The money is going out of the pocket, also with a will of its own. Ritwik is down to the last five rupees—just enough for a bottle of Bangla—when he sees something from the corner of his eye.'

My friend punished the waiter for eavesdropping by sending him off for another drink.

'Now, Ritwik is a tall man, about six-one without his stoop. He can see above the heads of the market crowd. What he has seen is another tall figure. He charges through the shoppers. "Hey Manik! Manik, hello!" he says, for it is none other than Satyajit Ray, also cast out to shop by Mrs Ray. "Manik! You! Here? How good to see you!" says Ritwik. "Uh ... hello," says Manik warily, because he knows Ritwik. "Oh listen Manik, will you do me a small favour?"

' "Er . . ."

' "No, no, I don't need to borrow money today. Just hold this little one for a second, I'll be right back." And before Ray can say anything Ritwik disappears, leaving him holding the baby.

'Half an hour passes. Ray is stuck to the spot. People recognize him of course, and they stop to say nice things about his films, start asking about his latest project, friendly Calcutta people, someone advises him about his *mise-en-scène*. The baby wets his shirt. Forty minutes, still no Ritwik, Ray livid. Already three people have asked him where his little girl's mother has gone. Just coming up to an hour ... and ... and Ritwik is back! Swaying a little but looking very happy.

' "Ah Manik. Thank you, thank you, was she all right?"

' "Uh . . ." Ray looks down at the wet patch on his shirt.

'"What? She peed on you? Bad girl!" says Ritwik. And then he frowns in puzzlement. "But, but why did she do that? . . . She hasn't seen your new film!"'

We laughed before drifting into a silence. The film critic knew the Ray family. He shook his head.

'That Oscar was his last gasp. It's a matter of time now, he's in deep coma. He's being kept alive completely artificially. Tubes and machines. He has had no awareness over the last three days.'

The rum found combustion with a quintessential Bengali sentimentality, nudging the storyteller from the irreverent to the maudlin.

'I wonder what Ritwik will say to Satyajit when they meet,' he sighed into his glass.

'Oh,' grinned the film critic, 'Probably ..."Ah, Manik! You're finally here! Say, can you do me a favour?" I mean, why change the habit of a lifetime just because you are dead?'

'At which point Manik will turn around and come running back to this world!'

I got home and, as on every evening, my mother was watching TV. But instead of the usual soap I saw the actor Om Puri bringing down an axe on a tree trunk. 'Nice cut, bad film,' I thought and then realized that tubes and machines had failed—I had just been participating in an early wake. Om Puri brought down the blunt axe again. It slid off the wood without a bite.

My mother said, 'He passed away at six this evening. They've announced it.'

The President

Every famous death brings with it an onslaught on the senses and from the next day the barrage would begin:

A national period of mourning would be declared, bringing flags down to half-mast all over the country. Over the next week every newspaper and magazine would carry obituaries, articles, assessments of the films, paeans to the great genius' multifarious talents as a director, musician, writer and graphic designer. The writing would range from shrill hagiographies to reverent farewells in low and sombre tones.

Clichés like 'multifaceted genius', 'towering personality', 'irreparable loss' and 'end of an era' would be repeated as if the writers were controlled by a dictaphone with a looped tape.

Doordarshan would have a non-stop broadcast of everything on or by Ray ever filmed. Famous film personalities from all over the world would send messages of condolence, as would some heads of state.

Satyajit Ray, the most deeply private of men, would have one of the loudest, most public funerals ever seen in India.

In my mind I hear someone, say a ten-year-old from the town of Calceta in Ecuador, asking me, 'So, who was this man? Was he The President? How come his death stops a city of twelve million for two days?'

He was a storyteller who told stories in pictures. He was a storyteller who didn't make up too many stories of his own. He mostly told other people's stories but he told them well, sometimes very well indeed. When he started he didn't know how to tell stories but he taught himself. He saw how some people in other countries told their stories and he brought back those ways with him.

At that time, no one in the land told picture-stories the way he did and people began to take notice. Then people all over the world became entranced by his storytelling. They gave him lots of prizes. In his own country his fame grew and grew.

By the time he died, he lived in a high house. And even though there were other storytellers by then, some better than him, yes, by the time he died, he had been the President of the Storytellers for many years.

The high house

I live close enough to Ray's house and even closer to Belle Vue Nursing Home where he spent his final weeks. Before the irruption of a new apartment block just outside my window, I used to have a direct view of the Intensive Cardiac Unit on the top floor of the hospital.

A few days before he died, in a flippant moment, I had imagined him leaning out of a window at night, no building between us. I imagined waving at him, making faces, making him laugh with a cheekiness I had convinced myself he craved, surrounded as he was by all those hush-voiced nurses and funeral doctors.

I am not normally given to sentiment, but the night he died I decided to walk over to Bishop Lefroy Road. Perhaps curiosity took me, or maybe some strange desire to pay my respects. Perhaps I thought I would meet up with one of my friends from earlier in the evening.

I walked out of my house into a strange landscape. All around me were signs of new construction. In many places the pavement had disappeared, buried under landslides of sand and stone chips. Streets dogs lay curled up under the bones of old buildings. Cement mixers stood gaping in their sleep, tired and still, as if they'd been dragged across the decades by some nineteenth-century time machine. Half-built apartment blocks teetered past dim new concrete caged by fragile grids of bamboo and rope scaffoldings.

Over the last two decades, the contractors and real estate operators had had a free run in this area, putting up new buildings wherever space could be made. One by one the old colonial houses had fallen, consigned to burial by a nexus of rich businessmen and apathetic government officials. More recently, similar transformations had begun taking place all over town. Between apathy and bribery some of the most beautiful parts of the city were brutalized with no benefit to anybody but the wealthy and the politicians.

The Calcutta of 1992 bore no relation to Kipling's 'city of dreadful night'. It was difficult to find traces of the other, graceful yet terrible, city that Tagore had written about. It was no longer the city that Ray had depicted so wonderfully in one or two of his early films.

In the sixties, Calcutta had been labelled 'the poorest city in the world' by the media and the aid agencies. And though, in the smog-ridden chaos, you could see the direct results of the that period, it was no longer 'the black hole of our times' either.

It was as if Calcutta was an actor. A quick-change artist who had sloughed off succeeding costumes, keeping an ornament from one, a torn rag from another, a gaudy smear of make-up from a third, while transforming himself before your eyes into a completely different character.

I had lived in Calcutta for most of my life and it was still my city, the only city in which I felt at home. But at thirty-two, I already caught myself relating to it with a deep uneasiness. For someone like Ray, the alienation must have been far more intense.

Despite the fact that most of Ray's successful films are not about the city, he was essentially a cosmopolitan man, also most at home in Calcutta. But the Calcutta that he loved, that had nourished his art in its formative stages, that city had done a disappearing trick long ago. The problem with the films Ray made after his first brilliant period, especially those set in the Calcutta of the sixties and seventies, was that he never actually came to terms with the changes taking place around him.

The house Ray lived in remained untouched by the metamorphosis of the surrounding area. But in his last years, all he had to do was to drive thirty seconds in any direction to be confronted by the upmarket concrete jungle.

The flat itself is in a lovely old building on the corner of two fairly quiet streets. The building was probably built early this century for Raj boxwallas. A stately staircase, an imposing door, high ceilings trapping beautiful light. Till recently, his study had a nice view of palm trees and other similar buildings. Living as I do, in one of the new concrete blocks, that flat, along with the already famous desk and armchair, was one of the few things I actually envied him.

As a 'marginal' filmmaker I couldn't claim even a fleeting acquaintance with Ray. But since Calcutta operates the way it does, I'd had the pleasure of entering the sacred lair twice or thrice. The first time was in the mid-eighties when I went to deliver an invitation to a screening of my first film.

Everyone knew that Ray very rarely ventured out to see films, especially documentaries by unknown young locals. I went, because that is what you did when you finished a film—you went and personally delivered the invitation to pay your respects, to ask for his blessings. The correct form for asking was tacit, because God help you if you did something as forward and stupid as people sometimes did, which is touch his feet. Ray came from a Brahmo background and the Brahmo distaste for Hindu melodrama coupled in him with a very English sense of decorum.

I went to the house just after Ray had been given the Legion d'Honneur by François Mitterand. I'd seen the ceremony on TV and it was still fresh in my mind: Ray dressed in *dhoti-kurta* approached Mitterand to receive the medal. Mitterand, shorter by a good few inches, put his hands on Ray's shoulders and pulled himself up, fully intent on delivering the traditional Gallic double kiss before parting with the gold. Ray, who had spent a lifetime turning down beautiful women wanting to kiss him, wasn't about to let this Frenchman plant his lips where no man had before. He gently parted Mitterand's hands from his shoulders and gave a small shake of the head. He then brought his palms together in a *namaskar* and bowed low—thus managing to duck any snipes Calcutta wits may have been about to fire at him.

I went to the house and tiptoed up the stairs. I knocked on the imposing cream-coloured door and waited. After what seemed like a very long time, someone opened the door. It could have been a servant, or a member of the family.

'Yes?' I stated my reason for disturbing. The door shut and I waited again. Another long wait before it opened and I was let in. I felt lucky, enormously privileged, and on a very short leash of time. I went past a screen into the study, a place I already knew from many photographs.

'Yes?' this time from a familiar voice that was nasal and deep at the same time. The reading spectacles came off the face and I was looked at. I was far too nervous to look back, or even look around. I did a minimalist folding of hands and ducking of head— because that was *de rigueur*—and then I stuttered out my business.

'Thank you. I am very busy with my next film and the doctors don't allow me to go out much, but thank you for the invitation.' I began my retreat. 'My best wishes.' And he turned back to his desk with the tilted illustrator's drawing board. The dismissal was, like the man, a polite one but no less firm for all that.

As I made my way down the stairs I remember thinking, 'This is how Mitterand must have felt.' I also remember thinking 'That wasn't too bad.' I was, in fact, relieved to have escaped the embarrassment of showing him this Early Effort. Later I would make other films, films that I wouldn't be shy about showing anybody. Only then would something else about that first meeting strike me—Ray's profound disinterest in work someone three generations down from him might have come up with. His complete lack of curiosity in a beginner's potential.

By the time my curiosity brought me to his house the night of the death, it was nearly midnight. There was a row of police vans parked nearby and someone had put up a bright 'wedding' light on a tree opposite the gate. A small crowd stood around, made up mostly of photographers. They were unusually quiet as they waited for the next celebrity to emerge. I noticed there were more cops than the people they were supposed to control. The crackle of the police radios drifted over from the parked vans, oddly out of place in the silence. The marriage foodlight threw strange shadows of trees onto the yellow walls—the kind of shadows you get when there is filming going on at night. Any moment I expected to hear a production assistant shout 'SILENCE!' or 'Shot over! *Jaan jaan, taara-taari chole jaan . . .*' letting passers-by through.

A tall thin man in a dirty white bush shirt and broken sandals sidled up to the police guarding the gate. He had his hands folded towards an officer. 'Please let me go upstairs. I know the family. He knew my father. And my mother too. He was like a god to me. Please, I just want to pay my respects. He knew me since I was a child. He was like an uncle. Please let me go up. What is this? Why are you doing this? I just want to pay my respects to his wife. I know the family.'

The officer ignored him, revelling in the fact that he had someone he could turn down, that at last he had something to do. The man, a decrepit looking forty, continued his refrain in a flat chant. His folded hands were pointing at the officer but his face was now turned away, trying to make eye contact with somebody else, anyone, who would listen to him. The officer, realizing he was no longer the centre of the man's attention, turned and snarled at him. The man backed away and fell silent.

It must have been difficult to deal with growing international fame in what was, in the fifties and sixties, essentially a small town containing a lot of people. The swarms of mediocrities trying to climb onto the bandwagon of greatness must have been tiresome and the reclusiveness, which grew over the years, must have seemed the only logical course to take. But on each of the three odd occasions I walked away from the most famous ivory tower in Calcutta, I couldn't help feeling that a large part of the 'grand recluse' persona was deliberately cultivated to add to the mystique and the power that came with it.

It was a Faustian pact and every great artist who has made that deal paid the price in the quality of his art.

I sometimes find myself comparing Ray and Picasso.

Both were young men with a certain sense of self-worth and a faith in their own destiny. Both came into their own when the umbrella of great predecessors blew away. In Ray's case, Rabindranath Tagore left behind a huge, deep footprint, and the artists of the next couple of generations floundered as they tried to climb out of its trench.

For Ray, following Tagore was a mug's game. As a writer, or even as a painter (Tagore began painting when he was nearly seventy), in the Calcutta of the late forties, sliding off the cliff-face of the Tagorean legacy was a very real danger. Ray had to take the ethos onto another plane and cinema presented the perfect space in which Ray could leave behind the trap of his enormous classical facility, that of language and the drawing line.

Both Ray and Picasso made a leap into the unknown and became famous for it. Fifty years after Picasso painted *Les Demoiselles d'Avignon*, 'The first painting of the 20th century', Ray completed *Pather Panchali*. The film became the one art product which kick-started newly independent India's life as a modern cultural nation.

Like Picasso, Ray followed his first success with prodigious output developing on that success. Like the Spaniard, Ray was very good with his hands and it showed in his work. But, again, like Picasso Ray could not find it in himself to deviate too much from the formula that brought him his initial acclaim.

Picasso was done with his truly great work within a decade or so of the beginnings of cubism. Within nine years of completing *Pather Panchali* in 1955, Ray had finished more or less all of his best work—the other two films of the Apu trilogy, *Parash Pathar, Devi, Teen Kanya* and, finally, *Charulata*. Picasso had the odd spark of Guernica. Ray had the brilliant expressionist explosion of *Goopy Gyne Bagha Byne* in 1968, after which he rode on the momentum of the earlier work. And though it was a great momentum, very little power was added by the remaining sixteen films.

Like Picasso, every mark that Ray made began to be regarded as brilliant. The few critical voices got drowned out in the chorus of 'Genius!' 'Maestro!' 'Greatness!' and that chorus seriously impaired Ray's ability to see the world around him. Towards the end he was prickly about the smallest criticism, even from old and close friends.

For Picasso the end came behind the electrified fence of his estate in Cote d'Azur, Ray, living in Calcutta, had little need for the extravagance of electric fences—the invisible wall that built up around him had a thick and effective coating of awe on the outside and an equally dense layer of arrogance on the inside.

In the deluge of mini-hagiographies that would come in the next few weeks there would be many hilarities. But, even among those, one would really stand out for its ignorant sycophancy: Raghubir Singh, a man best known for a series of banal coffee-table photo books, would spout on about Ray as 'a true *flâneur*'.

As I stood in front of his house the night of his death, I remember wondering when the last time was that The President had walked around his kingdom incognito. Judging by the films you could be forgiven for putting it as sometime in the sixties, a quarter century before he died.

The gates opened to let a car out. The flash-guns sparkled briefly. The gates shut and the man in the dirty white shirt was back, now in front of another policeman. He began his mantra again. Maybe he really knew Ray, I thought. No, he would have sent up a note. Someone leaving would have noticed him. Even through the crust of self-importance that people acquire when organizing the newly dead, someone would have called him up . . . but then again, maybe not. This man was not a character from a Ray film. He had a dangerously cloying quality about him, something obsessive, a man wanting a slap, violence, anything to break through to some attention, some human contact. An extra out of somebody else's film who had wandered onto the wrong set.

The set

The first time I saw the great man was on a set in Indrapuri studios. I had just come out of school and decided I wanted to be a filmmaker after seeing Antonioni's *The Passenger*. Subsequently I'd managed to see one or two of the Apu trilogy with the gaping awe they deserve from any seventeen-year-old.

At the time I had a silly idea that my ambition was unique among people my age. I was actually part of a very common phenomenon. In Ray's time, career ambitions for teenagers of artistic bent had ranged from wanting to be a poet like Rabindranath Tagore to wanting to be a painter like Rabindranath Tagore. By the time I began college that had changed. In large part because of Ray himself, every third boy or girl in Calcutta now wanted to become a film auteur.

Ray was, at the time, shooting *Shatranj ke Khiladi*. Richard Attenborough had come all the way from London to play General Outram. The Nawab of Awadh was being played by Amjad Khan, fresh from his success in *Sholay*. Other stars included Shabana Azmi.

I knew someone who knew someone who knew the sound recordist and managed to get into Indrapuri to watch the shoot.

Indrapuri is one of the five studios in Tollygunj, Calcutta's studio-*para*. Entering it for the first time you felt as if you were being led into a decrepit castle. Big rusted steel gates opened to let you into the first courtyard where the cars parked. Then, after your provenance had been thoroughly checked, you went through another gate into the compound where the big hangar-like sound studios were. Outside the studios people milled about—extras, technicians, labourers, sundry others who go into making the small army that supports a major production.

In the studios that were 'off' that day, local carpenters and painters—some of the best set-makers in the world—worked away at creating bits of nineteenth-century Lucknow out of plywood, clay and plaster. The studio in which the unit was filming sprouted a small crowd around the doors—people craning their necks over each other's shoulders, peering into the cavernous inside to try and catch a glimpse of the action.

Though I didn't know it then, I had come to watch Ray filming what many would consider to be his last good film.

The year was 1977. Ray's old rival Ghatak had died the year before, the alcohol finally taking its toll. He died having made only five full-length films and several incomplete or unrealized projects. It would take another decade before people began to realize what they'd lost in Ghatak's early death.

By 1977 Calcutta was no longer the only city which pro-duced serious cinema. The 'New Wave' of art films was firmly established in Bombay and in the south of India. In Bengal, the violent upheavals of the sixties and mid-seventies—the Naxalites and the Bangladesh war followed by the Emergency—had left deep scars. The damage was both economic and spiritual. The Left Front led by the CPI(M) had just assumed power and it would stay in government for a period of twenty years, a stretch still far from over.

The Leftists couldn't, by themselves, have created the intellectual impoverishment of Bengal. But, as they did with the economic poverty they inherited, it was something they used for their own ends.

Across this time there would be a surreptitious but sus-tained undermining of traditions, histories and ideas that didn't fit into the Leftists' vision of a 'revolutionary' future. At the same time, as the walls got covered with the hammer and sickle and portraits of Marx, Lenin and Stalin, businesses and industries would be wooed back to the state they had abandoned in the sixties.

The new Bengali culture emerging from this mix would have little to do with the ethos of Tagore or the films of Ray. In turn, Ray's own work would never be able to capture the cruelty and barrenness of spirit that a dismemberment from cultural memory brings about. To find a reflection of that tragedy in the cinema, people would have to go back to Ghatak's films—where the future was already, startlingly, anticipated.

Contemporary Bengali films in the eighties would suffer from the intellectual poverty of the milieu they came from. The new pretenders would produce films at a regular rate but nothing would emerge from their cameras to challenge Ray's best or Ghatak's. On the surface, these middle-aged 'young turks' would take on radical postures but the pith and spirit would be absent.

Politically, Ray was always regarded as a weak liberal. His films rarely made overt political statements and when they did, they were watery and extremely naive. Ghatak had broken away from the Communist party in the fifties and the Leftist establishment would remain uncomfortable with his legacy. His scathing attacks on any humbug, whether it came from the Right or his old comrades in the Left, would remain difficult for many to forgive or forget.

The 'young turks' of the eighties would prove far more palatable to the Government. They would go into all the required jargon of committed Leftist filmmakers but there would be nothing really disturbing or challenging either in the form or the content of their tepidly conceived films. The Left establishment would find them unobjectionable. The Right, growing in power across the country, wouldn't be particularly bothered by them either.

By 1977 Ray, like De Gaulle, was neither to the Right nor the Left, he was 'above'—stuck carrying the baby of fame. Whereas Ghatak had spent years between films teaching younger filmmakers, Ray was known for keeping his distance from other directors. He regarded them either as beneath him or as competitors, quite often both. And whenever he imagined any danger to his ambitions he also had the power to put others' careers on pause.

Years later at a party, I got into a conversation with a well-known director who was not from Calcutta. I knew he had struggled through the seventies despite considerable talent. Besides his talent, I knew the man for his formidable erudition—he was normally a man who carried a big intellectual stick but spoke softly. We were talking about Tagore, Ray and Bengali insularity in general when, with sudden tears in his eyes, he burst out at me. 'Do you know your Mr Ray stopped me from getting any money for my film—for seven whole years? All he had to do was to keep quiet, to not object. But, because I was a pupil of Ritwik's, because, as a student, I'd once criticized Ray in print, he let it be known that I didn't know how to make films. And that was it. All doors were shut as far as government funding went. That was your great Mr Ray.'

He wasn't my Mr Ray and it was a completely believable statement. Over the years, as I got more and more involved with cinema, I would hear a lot more about this side of Ray and I wouldn't be able to put down too much of it to jealous backbiting. But on my first day inside Indrapuri studios I didn't know any of that—I was entering the magical circus of film-making and I had no sense of the grime and sadness that lay just behind the glowing tent.

Inside the studio, even on a hot day, the punch of extra heat from the lights was a shock. The paint from the movable walls of General Outram's office gave off a smell reminiscent of Durga Puja *pandals*. Indeed, the whole thing had the feel not so much of a circus as a religious ceremony.

There were several minor gods—Richard Attenborough in a plumed hat, the equally handsome Victor Bannerjee and Tom Alter, their good looks rebounding off each other like a rally between Sampras and Agassi, the unseen presence of Shabana

Azmi, Sanjeev Kumar and Amjad Khan emanating down from the dressing rooms. But my chief memory is that there was only one person who mattered on the set.

No matter where you were, no matter how crowded the space, you could always find your bearings by looking for that patrician head floating like a Himalayan peak above storm clouds. The controlled chaos revolved around the man they called Chhawphut—'Sixfoot'. Ray stood about eight inches taller than anybody else on the set and the ongoing madness never seemed to rise above the height of his shoulders. He was the fulcrum on which the mood of the place balanced.

If he was quiet then everybody spoke softly. If he gave a command, squads of sweating men jumped to it, moving the camera, laying tracks, moving lights. Ray himself oscillated between stillness and a pouncy energy. It was studio lore that he did everything himself, and I could see that he did. He hunched over Attenborough and conferred with him, he towered over both Alter and Bannerjee, two tall men, and gave them instructions, he called up to a light-boy to shift the throw of a light on a wall, he went back and moved a paperweight on Attenborough's desk by half an inch. Then he twisted nimbly through two chairs and went to the camera. He sat down, coiling himself around the blimped old monster, and glued his eye to the viewfinder.

'I am ready,' he called out, in a voice made for command, not too loud but sharp enough to cut through the hubbub. It was as if he'd gently nudged a domino. A series of assistants relayed the word all the way from the centre of the universe to well outside the doors of the sound stage.

'Okay. Taking. Silence please.' Another relay of 'silence', the word mutating from Ray's clipped English down the hierarchy, ending up as a bellowed 'SAAILAINSH!' under the noon sun in the compound, freezing *samosas* in the half-open mouths of extras, cups of tea scalding technicians' lips in mid-sip.

The art theatre

The day after Ray died was typical for April in Calcutta. Hot, flat light from a lightly overcast sky, muggy. The kind of day people hate shooting on.

The body had been moved to the Nandan film theatre and put under a shamiana constructed over the open space at the entrance.

The theatre is the centrepiece of the art film complex built by the Communist state government. Completed in 1984, it was named by Ray and the logo was also designed by him. When it first came up, Nandan was memorably and precisely described by a wit as 'a Stalinist-Victorian corset'. Though not as forbidding as some of the other buildings put up by the Left Front government, Nandan's stodgy shape remains an appropriate symbol for the official cultural policy—pompous on the outside, shoddy and hollow on the inside, and the whole thing deadeningly unimaginative overall.

By the time the theatre was built, Ray, his 'aboveness' notwithstanding, had become a mascot for the government. In 1955, Ray had managed to complete *Pather Panchali* because of an intervention by B.C. Roy, then the Congress Chief Minister of the state. Roy had ordered the Home Publicity Department to provide funds after seeing some of the sequences. The Congress had always reaped whatever mileage it could from this. The Communist Party of India (Marxist), then the chief opposition party, had been vociferously critical of this 'bourgeois' director and his 'reactionary' liberal humanism.

But those days were quickly forgotten once the CPI(M) came into power in 1977. Cinema was the revolutionary art and Ray was still the only Indian seeded among the world's top ten directors, next to the likes of Welles and Renoir. The CPI(M) was not about to let this Manik, this jewel, fall from its cultural crown. Ray not only designed the logo for the art film theatre, he also inaugurated it.

Looking at Nandan that day, I couldn't help feeling that the building had been designed not for Art Cinema but specifically for this grand public mourning.

The scene was certainly not from one of Ray's films. A long snake of people filed in past the bamboo barricades that had come up overnight. By eight o'clock the queues already stretched, sweltering, for half a mile in either direction of the gates. The traffic had already begun haemorrhaging—even by Calcutta standards a complete mess.

Nandan was a transformed space. The corners of The Corset were normally reserved by young lovers for their furtive trysts. That day every nook and cranny was stuffed with policemen. The railings next to the moat, usually marked out by geriatric film critics, creaked that morning from the weight of housewives and school groups.

I could see a graduated change in facial expression depending on where you were in the file. Furthermore away, there was resignation and boredom. People looked as they do in queues for voting booths at election time, as if they were there to do an unavoidable chore. As the file got closer to the body, there was a mixture of befuddlement and awe in the craning of necks. Someone occasionally folded their hands in a *namaskar*, somebody lifted her small child up to let him catch a glimpse of History, every now and then somebody wiped away tears.

In the queue moving away from the body there was a sense of relief, almost of triumph. It is an expression I suddenly remembered from my schooldays, when we were taken to see a piece of moon rock brought back by Apollo astronauts. At the exit, I remember being given a button which said I HAVE SEEN THE MOON ROCK.

Charulata's bed

An acquaintance, a designer from Haryana, put it succinctly a few weeks before the death: 'Satyajit Ray', he said 'is a city around which the Bengalis have built their intellectual slums.'

Perhaps. Satyajitnagar, a newer, and initially smaller, twin city of Tagorenagar, now fast outstripping the older town in growth, squalor and disastrous planning, is a sad image but one that makes sense.

Ray left Calcutta in 1940 when he was nineteen, to enter Tagore's university at Santiniketan. About a year later, Tagore passed away. At the time, Rabindranath's death was regarded as the terminal punctuation mark of a great 'golden' period, the end of Bengal's cultural reign over the rest of India which began in the mid-nineteenth century, with what is called the 'Bengal Renaissance.'

Calcutta had also come to a standstill when Tagore died. The funeral procession stretched for several miles and the grief at the passing of this old man touched many different corners of the country. Even outside the eulogies there was a real sense of losing someone who could never the replaced.

But, within twenty-odd years of this massive death something strange would happen in the public mind. A society obsessed with its culture would need another icon and Tagore's mantle would be taken out of the museum of memory. Over the space of a decade it would be fitted onto a pair of reluctant shoulders. The shoulders belonged not to a writer, nor a poet or a painter, but to a filmmaker.

Ray's best films either came from Tagore's novels and stories or were heavily informed by the world view that Tagore represented. There were few figures that could inspire humility in Ray. There were Beethoven and Mozart, there were a couple of Italian renaissance painters, but the first, and the only Indian and the only figure from recent times, was Rabindranath. Apparently, whenever someone was unwise enough to compare him to his hero Ray would show deep irritation. But out of his earshot Bengali culture continued to treat him as Tagore's successor.

Sometime around the early sixties Satyajit Ray began to

serve a sentence which was initially pronounced by international critical acclaim and then enforced by local adulation. He would serve this sentence till the day he died and well after. In a very different part of the same celluloid jail, concurrently serving a very different kind of sentence, was Ritwik Ghatak.

Between these two sentences lies the story of the death of culture. The boy from Calceta, Ecuador, pops up again. 'Who is this other guy? What was he to The President? Why do you keep bringing him up?'

They were both storytellers. One became famous because he told stories in a simple way. The other storyteller knew that the stories of his land were not simple. He tried to find other ways to tell them, and sometimes he did.

The one who became world famous made clear pictures of other people's stories—he was a great illustrator. The other one, whose stories few people understood at first, was different. He made pictures you had to look at again and again before you could get the story. You had to be patient and people weren't patient—they had developed a taste for world champions. They were bored with the home, they wanted the world. They weren't about to pay much attention to someone who couldn't show his stories around the world, in Venice, in Berlin, in beach resorts in the south of France.

They forgot that their first champion, the poet, became world famous because he didn't worry about the world.

The story is that both the storytellers lost their stories. They both died of heart failure. One because he couldn't find the simple stories to move his heart anymore. The other because his heart moved too much and no one wanted to listen to that movement—it was too painful and complicated.

'What?' says the boy, but let's leave him behind for now, because there is another story.

Sitting in Olympia, a few days after the death, a friend, a filmmaker working in Tollygunj, asked me a question.

'Do you remember the bed in *Charulata*?'

Based on a Tagore novella, *Charulata* is, for many people, Ray's best film. Set in 1879 it is, on one level, the story of a triangular relationship between an upper-class intellectual, his young wife and his cousin. On another level it is a complex chamber piece, a miniature portrait of a time of great upheavals. It is also an amazing film for the way in which every element of cinematic art comes together to form a temporal work which challenges the best of music.

Ray was working at the absolute peak of his powers and so were the other two men who had journeyed with him from being rank beginners to masters. Subroto Mitra was shooting what was to be his last but one film for Ray before they split up. He delivered a bravura performance and Ray would never again achieve that fine dance between his camera and his actors. Bansi Chandragupta, the art director, also outdid himself in capturing the details of the period.

Some of the best moments in the film take place between the bed, Madhabi Mukherjee as the young wife Charulata, and Subroto Mitra's tracking camera. The bed itself is the kind of small aircraft carrier that all but the poorest Bengalis build their lives around even today. Of course I remembered the bed in *Charulata*.

'Do you know that bed is still in service in Tollygunj?'

'Really?'

'Yes, every rape scene in every B-grade movie or TV soap is filmed on that bed. I'm not joking. Come the day of shooting the scene the director yells "Go and rent Charulata's bed!" If someone else is doing their rape on it, they postpone and shoot something else.'

It was exactly the kind of irony Ritwik Ghatak might have appreciated. For me, the bed symbolized the fact that Ray had died in a world that you could still recognize from Ghatak's film of thirty years ago. A world galaxies away from Ray's own little universe.

Gulliver

At Nandan, the body itself did look like it had arrived from another planet. It was a long body, six feet-four inches to be exact, and it looked tied down by all the flowers and wreaths. I couldn't help thinking of Gulliver washed up on the beach with swarms of tiny Lilliputians twittering malevolently around him.

On one side of the body was a pyramid of photographers, their numbers swollen from the night before. They climbed and toppled over each other, subsiding for a few moments, then rising again in a noisy, hungry pile the moment another celebrity appeared with a wreath. Toes teetering on chairs, hanging off the supports of the shamiana, elbows in each other's lenses, their greedy faces looked like something out of a Fellini film.

On the other side were relatives, and people from his film unit, trying to cope with the constant deluge of flowers, replenishing the ice under the body, ushering in the VIPs. There were more politicians here than you would find at an Independence Day parade. And more policemen than at a test match in Eden Gardens. Whatever the species of police, the higher their rank, the closer they were to the body. They looked officious and alert. 'For what?' I thought, 'Too late my dear Lestrade!'

The cops were trying to be kind and efficient but all they managed to do was create the feeling that it was, in fact one of their own Commissioners lying in state and you were here purely on sufferance.

Outside these kinds of occasions, the police in Bengal had a tough job to do and they didn't always do it well.

Since the CPI(M) had come to power thugs previously associated with the Congress party had defected to it, swelling their once disciplined cadres. The Left Front hadn't minded. It was better to have the young hoods in the tent passing out rather than the other way around. Besides, they were useful, nor just in maintaining loyalty at election time but even on a day-to-day basis. At first this policy had worked.

Across the eighties, 'Boys' Clubs' became an alternative to the police, another arm, through which the Left Front could keep local control. Every village in Bengal, every slum-*basti* in the Calcutta hinterland, sprouted little tin-roofed huts. These huts became centres from where everything from marital disputes to 'fund-raising' for the Puja celebrations was decided. The police were told to look the other way, to keep their hands off all but the most serious crimes committed by the boys of the Party. 'If there is a problem we will discipline them' was the line. But by 1992 a whole new generation of boys had grown up into this 'club culture' and they were not going to be easy to control.

These weren't the young idealistic Naxalites using violence for Revolution. Nor were they the local toughs of the seventies who ran film societies and drinking dens side by side, who reputedly appreciated the finer points of Polanski's films and Pelé's football. These were young men who could rape and kill and maim as a matter of habit. These were the representatives of another Bengal, a Bengal that didn't give a shit about Tagore and one Satyajit Ray.

This new Bengal would also pay its respects later that day, but at Nandan that morning, the last rites for the old Bengal were firmly in the hands of the authorities.

I began to play a game in my head. I began trying to find sequences from different film directors in the mêlée around me.

Khaki and *khadi*, brown and crisp white, mingling, conferring and parting in a constant waltz around the body. Put in some smoke, a fugue by Chopin, add a white horse and an old man sweeping up broken bottles, and you had a scene from Wajda's *Ashes and Diamonds*.

Inside the foyer, behind the shamiana, the pace was slower but no less feverish. Actors, directors, film bureaucrats, more relatives and politicians. There were several video cameras and tape-recorders. There were several video cameras and tape-recorders with 'great names' taking their turns in front of microphones. A few were genuinely reluctant, some were made inarticulate by grief but many were quite enthusiastic.

A young journalist stood in a corner mimicking the various celebrities.

A well-known director—

'Goutambabu please say something!'

'*Ki aar bolbo. Ekta Adhyay Shesh.*'

'In English please, Goutambabu, this is for the national television network!'

'Oh. What can I say. It is the End of an Era.'

A famous old actor—

'Please believe me, at this point I have just nothing to say, words fail me . . .'

Half an hour later, when he finishes it was only because the tape had run out.

Another famous director—

'Once Manikbabu and I were in Berlin together and his son got into my taxi . . .'

A track shot from one to the other. *The Discreet Charm of the Film Community* by Luis Bunuel.

A track out of the theatre's side entrance onto the bridge over the bright blue moat. A hard-faced Congress leader sweeping past, Count Dracula in a crisp *dhoti-kurta*, his entourage of minor vampires coming behind him, each carrying wreaths with slogans on them. Buddhadeb Bhattacharya, the Left Front government's state minister for Information and Culture, watches the opposition file in. There is a genial look on his handsome face—a mild-mannered Marlon Brando. He greets the Congress leaders and makes them an offer they can't refuse. Softly, with warmth, he says 'We are planning to leave for the cremation at 6 p.m.—and tomorrow a condolence meeting, all of us together.'

Back outside, a scene straight out of a Ghatak film: two cleaners from Nandan stand looking at the queues stretching in every direction. One of them says, 'Pity we are so stupid. If only we'd thought of it yesterday. A few hundred rupees worth of flowers . . . can you imagine the sales we could have had?'

The End

Behind Nandan, the trucks were being prepared. The one that would carry the body to the crematorium had its Tata-Mercedes snout hidden by a huge roundel of white flowers. A man was stringing yellow garlands across the windscreen. It looked like a hard-faced bride being hidden behind ornaments before her wedding.

On the side of the truck hung a sign, white letters on black, two words in Bengali which could be translated either as 'Satyajit is Forever' or 'Satyajit belongs to Eternity'. Either way, it looked like a billboard advertising an insurance scheme, or perhaps diamonds.

A statue of Tagore turned its back on the trucks and looked west into the sunset. I wondered what he would have thought of Ray and of the circus of his death.

Since I couldn't ask him, I asked myself—what was lost with this man's passing?

For me there was a feeling of losing a beautiful and familiar handwriting, the loss of a way of forming letters, words, passages, and despite everything, the sense of gentleness, of grace that the movement of that hand represented. I had never wanted to mimic that calligraphy, but my pen was free to find its own meandering partly because someone, this man, had marked his paper in the way he had. For that I was grateful.

A few days later a venerable Bombay critic would end his eulogy by saying, 'Thank you Master, for everything.' I could only say, 'thank you, for your best.'

A writer, beginning to be known for his novels in English,

had said to friends, 'Ray makes me proud to be a Bengali. He makes me proud to be an Indian.' Since I'm not a Bengali, the first was not a cross I had to carry. As for being a Calcuttan, or an Indian, the memory of Ray would never be protection against the uneasiness that I felt about my city and my land. By the end of 1992 both would be taken over by street thugs for a few weeks. The first indirect and hilarious portent of this would make the front pages the next morning.

In a little while Satyajit Ray's body would be lifted onto the truck. The police would swing into action clearing a path through people who by now spilled on to the roads. The cortege would leave Nandan and head south to the Keoratolla crematorium near Kalighat. The crowds of people would follow the official vehicles, singing Tagore songs, songs from Ray's own films, prayers.

When Tagore's body was taken to Keoratolla people had tried to tear off hair from his beard to keep as mementos. A young student, down from Santiniketan to pay his last respects, had had his pocket picked. Ray has recounted how he had to walk all the way to his mother's house because the pickpocket had made off with his bus fare.

Tagore had died in gentler times. That evening at the crematorium, a drunken thug called Sridhar would make his way through the police cordon to stand next to Ray's body. When asked to move, he would push Buddhadeb Bhattacharya, Minister of Culture and second in command of the state government. Bhattacharya would shout at the policemen to do something. As Sridhar would be dragged away, he would call out 'Saha-da! Saha-da!' appealing to the Police Commissioner of Calcutta B.K. Saha for help. It would come out that Sridhar was acquainted with the top-ranking police officer of the city. The police commissioner would be relieved of his duties.

I didn't see this happen, I only read about it in the newspapers the next day.

As preparations were being made to move the body from
Nandan, I turned away. I knew whatever happened, Ray would
have cringed if he'd seen the B-grade movie his funeral had
become. And if he met Ritwik Ghatak he would not turn back, I
knew he would prefer Ritwik's company over coming back to
this.

I headed north to Park Street and Olympia. The boy from
Calceta followed me, asking questions. I took him along. I had
no qualms about taking children to bars.

(November 1997)

SUKETU MEHTA

Bhopal Lives

B hopal has joined the roster of internationally recognized symbol-places, along with Hiroshima, Auschwitz and Chernobyl, whose very names have become synonymous with the tragedies that have taken place within their precincts. Mention Bhopal to people outside India, and they won't think of a graceful city on the hills above two lakes with some of the most glorious Muslim architecture in India. They will think about what happened on the night of December 2 and the early morning of 3 December 1984, when an accident at a chemical plant owned by Union Carbide of Danbury, Connecticut, led to history's worst industrial disaster.

On that night, as a deadly cloud of gas leaked from the factory and spread out over Bhopal, Nirmari, heavily pregnant, woke up to find herself alone. Her husband had taken their children out of their shack and begun running, like the rest of the city. But then the police, who were passing by, took her out on the road and gave her water. She started running too. Nirmari came to a field and began coughing and vomiting, so much that she felt that the child would come up out of her throat. Other women around her, almost of all of whom had delivered their babies at home, knew what to do. They pressed down on her stomach. And out came a baby girl. Later, when the father came back, there was the question of what to call her. 'She has been born on the night of the gas,' he said. 'So we'll call her Gasdevi.' The gas-goddess.

On that same night, in the same slum Panobai, who was also pregnant, was also running. She and her husband, too, had become separated, and Panobai, panting, blinded, sat down in a ditch, unable to run anymore. Some people noticed her, lifted her, and took her to a manger, where the lowing cows were tied up. In the barn, at around 2 a.m., on the December night when no stars could be seen, a baby boy was born. Panobai's eyes were huge, inflamed and burning, and for four days she did not see the being she had given birth to; she only felt him suckling at her breast. Then a volunteer team came around to give bread, milk and medicines. One of the volunteers was writing a prescription for the newborn. His pen was poised over the paper. 'Name?' he asked. Panobai shook her head. 'Well,' said the volunteer, 'since he was born on that night, we'll call him Jaharlal.' Poison-lord.

Everybody in Bhopal knows exactly how old Gasdevi and Jaharlal are, and will always know. Gasdevi is a smiling girl with two ponytails who hasn't a clue about the gas called methyl iso-cyanate, Union Carbide and the whole mess. She's in school now, in the third grade, and seems to be healthy. Jaharlal, on the other hand, is a terror, not afraid of anybody, picking fights even with his teachers. His mother says he's thin and not in good health, but he, too, knows little about the poison cloud that gave him his name. Jaharlal and Gasdevi are good friends, and they play together in the lanes of the slum and the fields nearby, always united in the mythic accident of birth, carrying no more memory of what happened than their names.

There is a pornography of images of disaster in the third world—famines, floods, war, earthquakes. Quick television interviews with the victims reinforce those images. And, as with all pornography, the net effect is this: the affected people lose their individuality, their humanity, and we, the viewers, who have no idea about their lives, begin to distance ourselves from them. As it is, they all look so foreign to us: all these brown or black people, poor things. So it is easy for us to forget them, as Bhopalis are now being forgotten.

A lot has been written about the bare facts of the Bhopal gas disaster: how it might have happened, how many died, how many were injured. What has rarely been portrayed is the complexity of people's individual responses to disaster. Not all in Bhopal passively accepted their victimhood. Many fought, and continue to fight, alone or in groups. And not all the people working for the giant corporation that caused this disaster erased the incident from their consciences. Ultimately, Bhopal is a tragic story, bitter and bloody, a tragedy that has brought out the worst in some people, yet offered the possibility of redemption for others.

A Carbide-commissioned study of the Bhopal disaster starts off by attacking the news media. It laments that journalists 'focus on the human interest aspects of the tragedy ... In recent years, the news media with their surfeit of investigative reporters have become a predictable presence at the site of an incident.'

Therefore, I must make my bias clear in advance: I went to Bhopal to focus on the 'human interest aspects' of one December night in 1984 during which, before the sun rose, several thousand human beings capable of love and anguish sank to their knees and did not get up again. By now, that night has claimed around 10,000 human lives and attacked in various ingenious ways at least another 300,000 human bodies. To my mind, this qualifies as a 'human interest' story.

The night of the gas

In May 1982, a Union Carbide inspection team from the Danbury headquarters visited the Bhopal plant and found sixty-one safety and maintenance problems, thirty of them major. A

series of gas leaks had already resulted in the death of one factory worker and several injuries. Five months before the night
of the accident, vital refrigeration and cooling systems had
been shut down. Around the same time, the maintenance crew
was reduced from six to two workers as part of a cost-cutting
drive. Local lawyers and journalists had been warning Union
Carbide for months that the plant could be dangerous to its
neighbours. The company responded that such fears were 'absolutely baseless'.

In the early morning hours of December 3, 1984, water
entered under still disputed circumstances an underground
storage tank containing 90,000 pounds of methyl isocyanate, a
highly toxic chemical used to make pesticides. This set off the
following reaction:

$$CH_3 NCO + H_2O = CH_3 NH_2 + CO_2$$

Forty-one tons of methyl isocyanate along with a stew of
other highly toxic gases possibly including hydrogen cyanide boiled
over and burst through the tank at a temperature of over 200
degrees Celsius and at a rate of over 40,000 pounds an hour. This
was the birth of what the scientists later named 'Bhopal toxic gas'.
The gas rose from the plant, then sedately, unhurriedly, floated
out over the sleeping city.

Bhopalis have very personal relationships with 'the gas'.
Accounts of that night—again, when people in Bhopal say 'that
night', they mean the night of December 2-3, 1984—describe
how the gas was going toward Jahangirabad or Hamidia Road;
how it hovered a few feet above the ground at some places or
how it hugged the wet farm earth in others; how it made all the
leaves of a peepul tree turn black and how it had a particular
hunger for the tulsi plant; how it would travel down one side of a
road but not the other, like rain falling a few feet from you while
you're standing in the sunshine. People know the gas like a member of their family—they know its smell, its colour, its favourite

foods, its predilections. One thing everybody remembers is the smell of chillies burning. Chillies are normally burned to ward off the evil eye, when, for example, a child is sick. People woke up and thought: it must be a powerful evil eye that's being driven away, the stink is so strong.

As people ran with their families, they saw their children falling beside them, and often had to choose which ones they would carry on their shoulders and save. This image comes up again and again in the dreams of the survivors: in the stampede, the sight of a hundred people walking over the body of their child.

Iftekhar Begum went out on the morning after the gas to help bury the Muslim dead. There were so many that she could not see the ground—she had to stand on the corpses to wash them. As she stood on the bodies, she noticed that many of the dead women had flowers in their hair. The gas had come on a Sunday, and people had dressed up to go out to a film or to someone's house for dinner. The women had braided their hair with jasmine or mogra—small, fragrant flowers.

When Iftekhar Begum came back from the graveyard, all her fingertips were bleeding, she had sewn so many shrouds.

On the day after the accident, propelled by a visceral, human impulse, Warren Anderson, Carbide's chairman at the time, flew to Bhopal to see the situation for himself and offer aid. He did this against the advice of his lawyers and public relations people and was promptly arrested, detained for several hours and put on a plane to New Delhi. He was granted bail and flew home a few days later. When he returned to Connecticut, Anderson met his real enemies—reporters, lawyers, shareholders and consultants, hounding him with questions, offering advice. He fled with his wife and his mother-in-law and holed up for a week in a Stamford hotel, having all their meals sent up—'a grown man hiding in a hotel room', as he later put it. After the accident, he had trouble sleeping. And well he might. Anderson is now wanted on charges of culpable homicide in India, and is rumoured to be living quietly in Vero Beach, Florida.

Arun's story

What would you do if you woke up one night when you were thirteen years old and, by the morning, seven of the ten members of your immediate family were dead? How would your life change? When I first meet the young man who I will call Arun, to whom this happened, he is busy writing a wedding invitation card. Not his own, not anybody's in fact; there will only be one copy of this invitation, and it will be shown to the judge in the gas victims' claims court. There is a Muslim woman with him. She was allotted Rs 50,000 (in compensation for her injuries) which the government has kept in a fixed-deposit bank account to prevent her from spending it all at once. To withdraw funds from her account, she has to demonstrate to the judge that she has some compelling need. Arun is wise to the inscrutable ways of the authorities; for a consideration, he will help her get her money out. So he sits next to me making up this invitation to a wedding that will never be.

Arun's fee for writing up the affidavit and printing one copy of the wedding card at a printing press (which costs him Rs 100) is Rs 3000. This, he points out, is less than what a lawyer would charge: 10 per cent, or Rs 5000. 'The lawyers hate me,' he crows.

The gas victim Arun loves his life. He wakes up at noon, massages himself with mustard oil, and spends the afternoon sitting on the newly-constructed balcony of his house, chatting with friends. In the evenings he drinks, or goes to the Hotel International and asks to see the 'special menu', which consists of several pages of pictures of the women they have for sale. On an occasional Sunday, he'll get partridges, which he kills with his own hands, cooks and shares with his friends, who seem to be in awe of him. Three or four times a month, he goes to the claims courts on behalf of someone. And that's enough money for him, mostly.

Arun first learned of the deaths of his parents and five siblings when he saw their photos stuck up on the wall by the side of the road. Till then people would tell him but he didn't believe them. Looking at the pictures the government had put up to alert survivors, Arun did not cry. Arun claims he has never once cried. 'There were so many corpses. Who will you cry over? After a while, the heart becomes quiet.'

On the night of the gas Arun fell in love. As Arun and his family ran, as one by one his parents, brothers, sisters dropped to the ground or got separated from him, Arun felt someone holding his hand and leading him. On they ran, through the chaotic streets. That was the beginning of Arun's first love. The girl holding his hand lived in his neighbourhood, and later on, she fed him and took care of him.

That girl was the first of his neighbours to adopt Arun and take care of him, but she was by no means the last. There were other families in the slum, his extended family in Lucknow, a rickshaw driver and his wife, and finally, the activist Satinath Sarangi, known with much love as 'Sathyu' among the survivors. Arun moved into Sathyu's house and became a poster child of the activist movement. His story was widely used, and he was recruited by all manner of groups, including the youth wing of the Communist Party of India, the state's major political parties and almost all of the activist groups working on Bhopal. Arun became a kind of travelling victim, going on tours to talk about the tragedy that had devastated his family, not only all over India but also, twice, to the United States. He was a natural. 'At the age of fifteen I learned to give such good answers that the journalists loved me,' he recalls gleefully. On one of his trips to the USA, Arun and a couple of the other survivors, while attempting to distribute literature in the Houston hotel where the annual meeting of Carbide's shareholders was being held, were arrested by the police and spent ten hours in jail. Arun was impressed by the fact that the American jail was air-conditioned.

But gradually, Arun went from being a victim to something of a predator. Sundry scams inevitably pop up in any community where a large amount of money enters the scene all at once, and Arun has learned how to profit from them. So, for a commission, using an efficient system of bribes paid to everyone from clerks to judges, Arun will extract the gas victims' compensation money from the clutches of the government. He is also a loan shark; he advances money at exorbitant rates of interest to illiterate migrants from the countryside, actively assists them in spending it in the Bhopal bars and beats them soundly if they cannot pay him back. He has a gang, which will assault people's enemies for a price. He points to my knee, Rs 300 for breaking that, and then to my arm, Rs 360 for that.

Once, when Sathyu was remonstrating with Arun about his misdeeds, Arun responded, 'Look at Warren Anderson. He got away with killing so many people. If he can get away, so can I.' Besides, Arun sometimes puts his potential for violence to good use. Though he is Hindu, he put his life on the line during the bloody Hindu-Muslim riots of 1992, when he stood guard outside Muslim homes with a sword.

Every year, on the anniversary of the gas leak, the chief minister holds a big commemorative public meeting and invites a number of victims. Arun will go this year and ask him for a favour—a coveted licence to sell kerosene, which he'll divert to the black market. The chief minister, he tells me with a laugh, will never refuse such a famous orphan anything when there are so many journalists present.

Arun hates the term 'gas victim'. Once, in 1987, when he and other survivors were travelling to a demonstration, the train stopped at a station and the loudspeakers boomed out. 'Now, all the gas victim children from Bhopal, go and play in the special waiting room.' Arun sought out the government officer responsible for the announcement and swore: 'Your mother's cunt.'

'Is it stamped on my forehead, gas victim?' he asks me. 'Should I beg for pity, Hai Allah, help me, give me some food, I'm a gas victim?' Arun instructs his kid brother: 'If a man thinks himself to be weak, he will be weak.' Accordingly, he insists the twelve-year-old boy get up at six every morning to do calisthenics. There is a reason, Arun believes, that he himself has remained strong. 'Gas? I shit gas out of my ass. You drink enough, you smoke enough, and there won't be any gas.' To prove that he is stronger than anybody, gas-affected or not, Arun steps in front of a passing minibus and looks at me. 'Shall I beat up the driver?' he asks.

But Arun also tells me, matter-of-factly, that he's been having *gabrahat*. This is a condition commonly reported by survivors. All of a sudden, Arun's heart will beat wildly, he'll start sweating and his mind will flood with anxiety. This lasts for about ten minutes. Since most of the people affected by the gas lived in the poorer part of Bhopal, they were, by and large, not deemed worthy of psychiatric treatment or counselling. It's certainly not anything the government will give Arun, or anyone, compensation for.

One night, three of us—Arun, his sidekick Ramdayal and I—sit in the gas victims' beer bar, a shed off the housing colony. Around us are gas victims, all of them men, drinking with the compensation money they should be spending to get treatment for their wives, education for their kids. As the evening progresses, Arun and Ramdayal are getting a lot more drunk than I am because they are drinking whisky-and-beer cocktails. Presently, they get into a theological argument: was God present on the night of the gas?

On the night of the gas, as his family was dying, as he was falling in love, Arun lost his faith in God. 'Mother's prick, six-seven people died—where the fuck was Ganesh? If I met him, I'd beat him with shoes and chase him off, mother's prick, sister's prick. The gas came, Ganesh fucked my mother, then ran away. If my mother were here I wouldn't have a history.' I've never seen him so angry; he's almost shouting and finally he becomes completely incoherent and the gaps between the obscenities vanish and it's all just obscenities: mother's prick, sister's prick. When he calms down, he says, 'Only work is karma, work is the fruit.' Later I realize what he's just said, in a single sentence: Krishna's teaching to Arjuna in the *Bhagavad Gita*.

The lifting of the veils

In the years after the poison cloud came down from the factory, the veils covering the faces of the Muslim women of Bhopal started coming off.

The Bhopal Gas Peedit Mahila Udyog Sangathan (the Bhopal Gas Affected Women Worker's Organization), or BGPMUS, is the most remarkable, and, after all these years, the most sustained movement to have sprung up in response to the disaster. The BGPMUS grew out of a group of sewing centres formed after the event to give poor women affected by the gas a means of livelihood. As they came together into the organization, the women participated in hundreds of demonstrations, hired attorneys to fight the case against Carbide as well as the Indian government and linked up with activist movements all over India and the world.

On any Saturday in Bhopal, you can go to the park opposite 'Lady Hospital', sit among an audience of several hundred women and watch all your stereotypes about traditional Indian women shatter. I listened as a grandmother in her sixties hurled abuses at the government. She was followed by a woman in a plain sari who spoke for an hour about the role of multinationals in the third world, the wasteful expenditure of the government on sports stadiums and the rampant corruption to be found everywhere in the country.

As the women of Bhopal got politicized after the gas, they became aware of other inequities in their lives too. Slowly, the Muslim women of the BGPMUS started coming out of the veil. They explained this to others and themselves by saying: look, we have to travel so much, give speeches, and this burqa, this long black curtain, is hot and makes our health worse.

But this was not a sudden process; great care was paid to social sensitivities. When Amida Bi wanted to give up her burqa, she asked her husband. 'My husband took permission from his older brother and my parents.' Assent having been given all around, Amida Bi now goes all over the country without her veil, secure in the full support of her extended family.

Her daughters, however, are another matter. Having married into other families, they still wear the burqa. But Amida Bi refuses to allow her own two daughters-in-law, over whom she has authority, to wear the veil at all. 'I don't think the burqa is bad,' she says. 'But you can also do shameful things while wearing a burqa.'

Half of the Muslim women still attending the rallies have folded up their burqas forever.

Sajida Bano's story

Sajida Bano never had to use a veil until her husband died. He was the first victim of the Carbide plant. In 1981, three years before the night of the gas, Ashraf was working in the factory when a valve malfunctioned and he was splashed with liquid phosgene. He was dead within seventy-two hours. After that, Sajida was forced to move with her two infant sons to a bad neighbourhood, where if she went out without the burqa she was harassed. When she put it on, she felt shapeless, faceless, anonymous: she could be anyone's mother, anyone's sister.

In 1984, Sajida took a trip to her mother's house in Kanpur, and happened to come back to Bhopal on the night of the gas.

Her four-year-old son died in the waiting room of the railway station, while his little brother held on to him. Sajida had passed out while looking for a taxi outside. The factory had killed the second of the three people Sajida loved most. She is left with her surviving son, now fourteen, who is sick in body and mind. For a long time, whenever he heard a train whistle, he would run outside, thinking that his brother was on that train.

Sajida Bano asked if I would carry a letter for her to 'those Carbide people', whoever they are. She wrote it all in one night, without revision. She wants to eliminate distance and the food chain of activists, journalists, lawyers and governments between her and the people in Danbury. Here, with her permission, are excerpts that I translated:

Sir,

Big people like you have snatched the peace and happiness of us poor people. You are living it up in big palaces and mansions. Moving around in cars. Have you ever thought that you have wiped away the marriage marks from our foreheads, emptied our laps of children, bathed us in poison, and we are sobbing, but death doesn't come. You have made us a living, walking corpse. At least tell us what our crime was, for which such a big punishment has been given. If with the strength of your money you had shot us all at once with bullets, then we wouldn't have to die such miserable sobbing deaths.

You put your hand on your heart and think, if you are a human being: if this happened to you, how would your wife and children feel? Only this one sentence must have caused you pain.

If this vampire Union Carbide factory would be quiet after eating my husband, if heartless people like you would have your eyes opened, then probably I would not have lost my child after the death of my husband. After my husband's death my son would have been my support. But before he could grow you uprooted him. I don't know myself why you have this enmity against me.

Why have you played with my life so much? In what way was I, a poor helpless woman, harming you that even after taking my husband you weren't content. You ate my child too. If you are a human being and have a human heart then tell me yourself what should be done with you people and with me. I am asking you only, tell me, what should I do?

Negative-positive

The gas changed people's lives in ways big and small. Harishankar Magician used to be in the negative-positive business. It was a good business. He would sit on the pavement, hold up a small glass vial, and shout, 'Negative to positive!' Then, hollering all the while, he would demonstrate. 'It's very easy to put negative on paper. Take this chemical, take any negative, put it on any paper, rub it with this chemical, then put it in the sun for only ten minutes. This is a process to make a positive from a negative.' By this time a crowd would have gathered to watch the miraculous transformation of a plain film negative into an image on a postcard. In an hour and a half, Harishankar Magician could easily earn fifty, sixty rupees. Then the gas came.

It killed his son and destroyed his lungs and his left leg. In the negative-positive business, he had to sit for hours. He couldn't do that now with his game leg, and he couldn't shout with his withered lungs. So Harishankar Magician looked for another business that didn't require standing and shouting. Now he wanders the city, pushing a bicycle that bears a box with a hand-painted sign: ASTROLOGY BY ELECTRONICE MINI COMPUTER MACHIN.

Passers-by, seeing the mysterious box, gather spontaneously to ask what it is. He invites them to put on the Stethoscope, which is a pair of big padded headphones attached to the Machin. Then the front panel of the Machin comes alive with flashing Disco Lights, rows of red and yellow and green bulbs. The Machin, Harishankar Magician tells his customers, monitors their blood pressure, then tells their fortune through the Stethoscope. The fee is two rupees. Harishankar doesn't like this business; with this, unlike his previous trade, he thinks he is peddling a fraud. Besides, he can only do it for an hour and a half a day, and clears only about fifteen rupees.

Harishankar Magician is sad. He yearns for the negative-positive business. Once the activist Sathyu took a picture of Harishankar's son, who was born six days before the gas came. He died three years later. Harishankar and his wife have no photographs of their dead boy, and they ask Sathyu if he can find the negative of the photo he took. Then they will use the small vial of chemical to make a positive of their boy's negative, with only ten minutes of sunlight.

The plague of lawyers

Almost immediately after the disaster, the American lawyers started coming, by the dozens. Out they stepped from the plane, blinking and squinting in the strong Bhopal light, covering their noses with handkerchiefs as they stepped gingerly though the dung-strewn lanes of the slums, glad-handing the bereaved, pointing to their papers and telling their translators to tell the victims, 'MIL-LIONS of rupees, you understand? MILLIONS!' And so the people signed, putting their names down in Hindi, or just with their thumbprints.

In the Oriya slum, eleven years later, word spreads that a visitor from America has come, and a cluster of people come to meet me. A young man, Bhimraj, and his mother, Rukmini, approach me hesitantly, holding out a carefully preserved piece of paper. 'The American government gave us this,' he says. 'Can you tell me what it says?'

I look at the document. It is a legal contract.

> *Contract between law office of Pat Maloney, PC, of the city of San Antonio, Bexar Country, Texas, and Suresh.*
>
> *Client agrees to pay attorney as attorney's fee for such representation one third (33%) of any gross recovery before action is filed, forty per cent (40%) of any gross recovery after the action is filed but before the commencement of trial, and fifty per cent (50%) of any gross recovery after commencement of trial.*
>
> *This contract is performable in Bexar Country, Texas.*

On the night of the gas, Rukmini abandoned her three-year-old son, Raju, who was dead, and ran with her five-year-old daughter, Rajni, who died three days later. When the lawyer came, they got Rukmini's husband, Suresh, to put his name down in Hindi on this document. They took the family's pictures. 'They didn't even send us a copy,' says Rukmini. That was the last the family heard from the man who they believed had come on behalf of 'the American government'. So now they ask me, what should they do with this paper that they've been holding on to for eleven years?

'Tear it up and throw it away,' I tell them. 'It's junk.'

They look at me, their faces blank, not understanding.

(When I returned to America, I tried to contact attorney Pat Maloney. He did not return my phone calls.)

Responding to such abuses, the Indian parliament passed a law declaring itself the sole legal representative of all of the Bhopal gas victims. It sued Carbide in Federal Court in New York. The court held that the proper venue for the case should be in India; spectators were treated to the uniquely edifying spectacle of hearing the Indian government's lawyers argue the inadequacy of its own legal system, countering Carbide's lavish testaments to the excellence of the very same system. The reason was simple:

everybody knew that any potential damage award given out by
the Indian court would be considerably smaller than an award by
a US court. Had the victims succeeded in suing the company in
its home country and winning, they would probably have bankrupted the giant corporation, much as the asbestos liability cases
bankrupted the Manville Corporation and breast-implant litiga-
tion bankrupted Dow Corning.

As it transpired, after prolonged legal wrangling, the Indian
Supreme Court unilaterally, without giving the victims a chance
to make their case, imposed a settlement to the amount of $470
million, with the government to make up any shortfall. The government had asked for $3 billion from Carbide. Carbide execu-
tives were delighted; they speedily transferred the money to the
government. That was in 1989. The first victim did not see the
first rupee of Carbide's money until the Christmas of 1992, eight
years after the night of the gas. A total of 597,000 claims for
compensation have been filed. As of May 1996, the government
has passed rulings on only about half of them, 302,422, and awarded
compensation for injuries to 288,000 Bhopalis. Out of the total
settlement amount of $470 million plus interest since 1989, the
government had, by May 1996, only disbursed some $241 million.

The quantification of loss

A government psychiatrist who has done a close study of the
minds of the gas victims has come to this conclusion: they don't
want to work. 'You can't get domestic help in Bhopal nowa-
days,' the doctor complained to me. 'If a family has five affected
people who get Rs 200 each (in interim relief), that's a thousand rupees a month, so they don't want to work.'

There is a widespread belief that the people destroyed by
the gas, who tended to come from the poorer section of Bhopal,
aren't receiving compensation that they are legally and morally
entitled to for grievous injuries, but some sort of unearned

windfall that has made them indolent. This belief is prevalent among the rich in new Bhopal, government officials and Carbide executives.

J.L. Ajmani is the secretary of the gas relief department of Madhya Pradesh, and he won't give me an interview. Ajmani is a man of the twenty-first century. In his luxurious office, he has a computer, a bank of three phones, a sofa, a huge desk and an executive chair in which he reposes under a big picture of Mahatma Gandhi. While brushing me off, he keeps tapping into his digital diary. I ask him about allegations of corruption in his department. He laughs fearlessly. 'It has been eleven years. Volumes have been written. You also write.'

Although the government isn't releasing figures about the average amount of awards, the welfare commissioner's office told me that the maximum compensation awarded for deaths is Rs 1,50,000 except in a handful of cases. Mohammed Laique, a local lawyer who has been representing claimants from the beginning, gave me the standard rates. For most deaths, the amount awarded is Rs 1,00,000. For personal injury cases, 90 per cent get Rs 25,000 (the award bestowed on most of the survivors I spoke to directly).

Of these amounts, said Laique, 'claimants lose between 15 per cent and 20 per cent at the outset in bribes. To get money out early, you pay another 10 per cent' ... Then there are sundry small bribes. Clerks in government offices demand anywhere from Rs 100 to 200 to move papers, depending on the size of the awards. The payments the government has been disbursing since 1990 for interim relief (Rs 200 a month) are also deducted from the awards. This means that from an award of Rs 25,000, the maimed survivor in September 1995 could expect to receive Rs 7,600.

Union Carbide claims that the compensation is 'more than generous by any Indian standard'. Is it really? For comparison, Laique pulls out the schedule of standard compensation set by Indian Railways for railway accidents, a common enough occurrence. The schedule is gruesomely specific:

In case of death: 2,00,000 minimum
For disability of one leg: 1,20,000
If one or two hands are cut off: 2,00,000
If one or two legs are severed: 2,00,000
Thumb cut off: 60,000
If four fingers cut off from one hand: 1,00,000
Three fingers cut off: 60,000
Two or one fingers cut off: 40,000
Breast cut off: 1,80,000
For problem with one eye: 80,000
Hip-joint fracture: 40,000
Minimum for bodily injury: 40,000

'And the railways give very fast decisions, plus interest after three months,' adds Laique. During the bloody communal riot-ing that followed the destruction of the Babri Masjid mosque in Ayodhya in 1992, the government gave a minimum of Rs 2,00,000 to the families of each person killed; these were peo-ple of the same socio-economic status as Carbide's victims. It's clear that, if a Bhopali had any choice in the instrument of his death, it would be financially much more advantageous to be killed or maimed in a train wreck or at the hands of a religious fanatic than through an American multinational's gas cloud.

In addition, all the potential victims have not yet been born. The Indian Council of Medical Research (ICMR), the gov-ernment body charged with studying the medical effects of the disaster, conducted detailed genetic studies on the survivors. Then the ICMR issued an alert: descendants up to the third genera-tion of the survivors may sustain genetic damage leading to cancer and abnormalities of offspring.

'Moral responsibility'

Anderson's 1984 Bhopal expedition marked the last time a senior Carbide executive from Danbury got his shoes soiled in the city.

In the years after the tragedy, Carbide has admitted 'moral responsibility' for the disaster. The company proposed various small projects to aid the victims, including setting up a vocational centre and contributing fifty-two million toward relief. After the assets of its Indian subsidiary were seized by Indian court, Carbide made a virtue out of necessity and, at the Supreme Court's direction, announced that it would use the frozen assets to set up a trust to build a new hospital for the survivors. The company refuses to use any of its unencumbered assets for this laudable endeavour.

Throughout, it has stoutly maintained that the disaster was a result of deliberate sabotage. The Carbide hypothesis goes like this: a disgruntled employee, upset about being demoted, deliberately introduced water into the methyl isocyanate tank, setting off the deadly chemical reaction. Subsequently, all the employees and supervisors on duty at the plant at that time decided, for reasons best known to them, to engage in a massive cover-up of the real causes of the accident, and have successfully maintained their conspiracy for eleven and a half years.

'Much of the world's safety engineering community doubts the veracity of Carbide's sabotage evidence', writes Wil Lepkowski, the American reporter who has most closely followed Bhopal, in *Chemical and Engineering News*. That evidence, Lepkowski points out, has never been subjected to scientific peer review or presented in court. Carbide will not name the saboteur, even though it promised to do so in court 'at the appropriate time'. That was in 1986; a decade later, an appropriate time has still not been found.

At the moment, there is no Carbide employee in Bhopal. There is no executive, no secretary, no engineer personally supervising the setting up of the hospital, nobody walking through the slums to make sure that the people they visited their holocaust upon are being adequately taken care of.

Carbide is doing nothing to monitor the settlement amounts, to ensure that the victims' financial needs are being taken care of; its labs are doing no research, nor is the company funding any, on

the long-term effects of methyl isocyanate; and there is no monu-
ment in Danbury or at any other company site to the gas victims
of Bhopal. As Carbide's chief of public relations Bob Berzok put
it to me when refusing my request to talk to anyone but himself
at the company, anyone at all from the president down to a caf-
eteria worker, 'This does go back ten years and I'm not interested
in disrupting the business going on here. I inquired of several
people and the feeling in general for those who were here ten
years ago was that there really was no interest in discussing their
personal feelings (about Bhopal).'

Berzok himself has been to India some fifteen times in
connection with the Bhopal disaster, not to help the victims but
to help the Indian subsidiary better manage its public relations.
Staying at the posh guest house that Carbide used to own in Shamla
Hills, Berzok has never once visited the slum colonies where the
victims live and die; and he doesn't recall a single name or a single
distinguishing feature of any of the victims. He saw some of them
in the medical stations in the old city. 'There were some people
that were having difficulties breathing,' is what he remembers.

For Union Carbide, Bhopal was a hit-and-run accident.

'I wanted him to apologize', says Syed Mohammed Irfan about
Warren Anderson. Irfan lost his sister and his health because of
the Carbide factory. Since the accident, his wife is terrified of
living in Bhopal and has left him to live elsewhere in the state. 'I
wanted him to apologize, be humble. Say we made a mistake; get
treatment, we'll pay for it. We wouldn't have hanged him.' This
didn't happen. Carbide may have accepted 'moral responsibility'
for the disaster, but has never apologized to the people of Bhopal.

So Irfan's views have changed. 'Now if I meet Anderson in
the street I'll kill him.'

I have also met people who don't think Carbide is to blame.
A high school teacher who lost her niece, and has seen her own
health suffer, told me, 'I feel no anger toward Carbide. It's the
fault of the technology.' All of Bhopal is not a vengeful mob

thirsting for revenge. Berzok emphasizes that whenever he was in Bhopal, travelling openly as a Carbide employee from the USA, 'I was treated very graciously, very hospitably, and that was true of all my visits over the years.'

Maybe if the victims saw their enemy in person, could put a human face on him, witnessed his genuine anguish and his tears, there could be some hope of forgiveness, or even of reconciliation. But as it is, the dehumanized structure of the multinational corporation works both ways; it makes it easier for individual officers of the corporation to avoid personal liability, and it makes it easier for outsiders to hate an abstract entity, a faceless monolith. Images of Anderson are drawn all over walls in Bhopal; they depict a stick figure with a top hat below the slogans 'Hang Anderson' or 'Killer Carbide'.

Sathyu once gave the children of the survivors in the slum where he lives pens and paper, and asked them to draw pictures of Anderson. I saw the children's drawings; most of them are depictions of the devil. But many of the horned figures are smiling and almost endearing, as if the young artists have not quite grasped the nature of evil.

Brian Mooney's story

In December 1984, Brian Mooney, one of six children of a Hackensack, New Jersey, shoe salesman, was working at the plush Park Avenue offices of Kelley Drye & Warren, 'with people who belonged to country clubs and played squash'. Kelley Drye, one of the oldest and most prestigious law firms in New York, was also Union Carbide's outside counsel. Mooney at the time was a few months out of law school, so when the Bhopal case broke, he was not one of the senior attorneys there. But the entire firm went into frenzied activity, with people working round the clock on the case. Mooney was put to work on legal research, principally insurance coverage issues. Every morning that December he would open the *New York Times* and read gruesome accounts of the dead and dying and then take the subway to Park Avenue to put in a full day's work preparing the defence of the corporation that had done this to them.

Mooney had to rationalize to himself the reasons why he was working for Carbide's law firm. It was, he says, 'a naive belief that people, especially people with suits on, are not capable of malice and wrongdoing especially on such a large scale.' Also, in this case, the opposing side, in the courts at least, was the Indian government, 'not a pristine entity either'.

But gradually Bhopal and other cases he was working on that were even more untenable personally dominated his thoughts. Mooney, who is gay and a former Catholic, used to celebrate mass on Saturday evenings at a Greenwich Village church with a gay Catholic group. New York's Cardinal O'Connor forbade use of the church for the services. So some of the spurned worshippers started going to St. Patrick's Cathedral on Sunday mornings, where, during the Cardinal's sermons, they would stand up en masse and silently turn their back on him.

The archdiocese of New York, through its legal counsel Kelley Drye & Warren, sued the protesters and obtained an injunction against them. A woman at the firm asked Mooney to serve the summons; he still isn't sure if she knew that he was gay, but he laughed and said absolutely not. She never spoke to him again.

Mooney slowly realized that he had no remaining faith in the legal system, that it had an inefficiency woven into its warp and woof. Mooney quit Kelley Drye in 1988. 'At the time, I didn't have any idea of what I was going to do; I was very good at not thinking about myself because of my being gay.' He was twenty-eight, and started to ask himself questions that a fourteen-year-old would ask, about the purpose, meaning and direction of his life. He knew that he wanted to help people, but he didn't believe law was the way to do that.

After a few years of drifting, Mooney applied to graduate

school at the University of Michigan at Ann Arbor for the doctoral programme in anthropology. He was accepted and given a teaching assignment with a salary equivalent to one-tenth what he used to make at Kelley Drye. In the summer of 1995, Mooney decided to go to Bhopal and study the effects of the legal system on the very people his former employer had commanded him to battle against.

One day that summer, Mooney found himself in the part of the gas-affected women, at one of their Saturday rallies. He was there in his role of anthropologist/observer, ready to note down what the women were doing, why they were here, the structures they lived within. Suddenly he felt a man tugging at his arm and heard an announcement to the effect that an American visitor would now be making a speech. Mooney was caught off guard and extremely uncomfortable. 'I shouldn't be speaking to them,' he thought. 'They should be speaking to me.' But he found himself, willy-nilly, thrust on to the speaking platform, with a mike in front of him.

Mooney began in his halting Hindi, then switched to English. He told the women that he was studying to be a teacher, and that the students he was teaching at the moment didn't know anything about the rest of the world and they didn't know anything about corporate ethics. These were students who would later go to work for companies like Union Carbide. He was here to gather their stories, he told the women, so he could relate them to his students, so that maybe those students, uniquely powerful because American, would think twice about how the decision they might make as corporate executives would affect the lives of people halfway around the world. That's why he was here, in Bhopal: to gather their stories.

Mooney stopped and looked at the crowd. They applauded politely, smiled, but they didn't really understand. His translator's English was inadequate, and Mooney was left feeling extremely awkward. But, he realized at the same time, he had done something very important for himself: he had just defined his mission, the precise way in which he could help other people. He had been forced to think, and had found an answer to the most universal and least asked of questions: What am I doing here?

A charge against earnings

If there's a happy ending to this story, it's for the Carbide executives and shareholders. Bhopal made the company prey to a takeover attempt a year after the disaster, which forced Carbide to divest itself of its consumer operations and concentrate on its highly profitable core chemical business. In the financial manoeuvres that took place during the takeover battle, Carbide gave its shareholders a $33 bonus dividend plus $30 a share from the sale of its battery business, and gave its top executives a total of $28 million in 'golden parachutes' to foil future takeover attempts.

Of the $470 million settlement, $220 million came out of Carbide's insurance. After news of the settlement, Carbide's stock actually increased $2 a share. If a person owning a single share of Carbide stock worth $35 in December 1984 had reinvested all dividends and distribution rights, that share would have been worth more than $700 a decade later. 'Clearly, by any objective measure,' says Arthur Sharplin, a management professor who studied these dealings, 'Union Carbide Corporation and its managers benefitted from the Bhopal incident. It is ironic that a disaster such as Bhopal [would] leave its victims devastated and other corporate stakeholders better off.'

Before Bhopal, the worst industrial accident in world history, Union Carbide was involved in the worst industrial tragedy in American history, the death in the 1930s of up to 2,000 of its workers due to silicosis during the building of the Hawks Nest Tunnel in West Virginia. Carbide makes no mention of that episode in its corporate histories.

When I went up to the Carbide headquarters in Danbury, Berzok proudly handed me an effusive Paine Webber report on the company, dated September 1995. It states, 'We reinstate Carbide as our number one major chemical stock idea.' Not once does the name Bhopal come up in the report.

(December 1996)

GAUTAM BHATIA

The Ambassador

The driver goes out to take a leak against the boundary wall. I poke my head into the cream coloured Ambassador Mark II 1967 model with sun visor for a short unshared moment of automotive bliss. The atmosphere inside is a rich texture of sights and smells. Red rexine stretches over the seats, the driver's odour permeates the inside like the smell of dung in a village lane. But this is the rich unmistakable aroma of summer sweat and saliva, a sort of heaving glandular stench of Punjab that hangs about the floorboards, penetrating the dashboard, even suffusing the fluffy white dog hanging from the rear-view mirror. The driver's toothpaste and shaving kit are clumped against the rear window, as if on a dresser shelf and a wet towel drapes the rear seat.

I get in and shut the door. Closing my eyes I take in the full impact of what it means to be an Ambassador in India. I open my eyes to find my fingers running across the rim of the steering, my feet have adapted to the worn out curve of the brake pedal, the body is arched in the ergonomic imprint of the driver's own back. Then leaning back against the plushness that comes with age, I look across the dashboard picture of Guru Gobind Singh staring benignly back at me. And do what every Indian child does when first placed in an automobile. I pretend I am at a busy intersection in Lucknow and blow the horn. I honk again. And feel an immense and instantaneous surge of happiness.

The driver manages to start the car a mile down the driveway, and with his hand permanently planted on the horn we go tearing along the road. The Ambassador is a heavy car, supposedly made of steel but weighted down like lead. In terms of speed and handling, it falls somewhere between the Saturn rocket and a camel, between a turbo jet and a donkey. It takes time to gather momentum. And when it does, the driver naturally hates to have that momentum broken, for it means shifting to low gear and starting all over again. So he devises a more economical game plan. He decides to stop or slow down only for those other things heaving about the road that are heavier than an Ambassador, like buffaloes and trucks.

The driver pulls the car into high gear and we go racing along down National Highway 37. From the back window the city fogs into an indistinct blur, the palace fortress assuming a hazy outline, till after a while nothing remains of the receding city. It is incredible what speed can do. The heady lightness of movement is exaggerated by a sandstorm that begins to blow in fluffy gusts, swirling the dirt on the windshield and limiting the line of sight to a mere two feet. The driver has the common sense and foresight to know that this is a fairly sparsely populated region of the country with no more than a thousand-odd villages spread throughout the district. And we know we are in the central tribal belt of the country because Ravi saw some women in grass skirts carrying spears, and Sheila said she was sure she saw some French tourists. Driving through the sandy haze, with no sighting of the passing fields or surrounding landmarks I feel like an astronaut hurtling through free space weighed down by nothing, nor even the gravity of my life on earth. Till a sudden jolt tells us that we are after all human beings—frail and gasping, prone to head colds in the summer and headlong collisions on the highway. We have encountered a black hole. The car jerks clumsily to one side and the engine dies with a sad long moan. Sensing that something is wrong the driver jumps out. Working his way through the sand dunes he finds himself near the bonnet, and feels the forty-year-old grille bent out of shape, the headlight splintered. Shocked and deeply saddened by the injury to a family member he recoils in grief, holding onto the broken dented bonnet for support. As the tears begin to gather he sees the cause of his distress; an even older bullock cart, the ancient messenger of rural India quietly creaking on undisturbed, adrift in the landscape.

As the bullock moves away into the middle distance of the sandstorm, there is a sudden subliminal connection between the drivers of the two vehicles. As if in a sudden spark—an electric moment when the two understand each other, as only Siamese twins can. The bullock cart is the Ambassador with the leathery hide of an animal, the Ambassador, the reluctant animal duplicated in steel. You feel it every day, wash it daily in the village tank, check its gums, water it, or hose it. Both will serve you as no human being can.

When it is weary after a summer morning's run to the market, or a long hot ride to the neighbour down the road you must give it a rest. Remove its bald tyres and let the body cool in the dark shade of a tamarind tree. Give it a gallon or two of Mobil 307 and talk to it or read it a short story from Automotive Digest. Watch, after some time the radiator will snort in your direction. At night even the eyes will blink and fuse in a recognition of your compassion. Before you know it the car will be your slave for the rest of its life, which, in any case, is a lot longer than yours.

The driver watches the slowly rising needle on the speedometer. At ten kmph he runs over a dog that strayed onto his path. It's a dachshund so no one is about to miss him. At twenty-five kmph he maims a young fellow appearing for his BSc. exam in the Life Sciences at the local polytechnic. But it's all right. He wouldn't have gotten a job anyway. At forty he is a menace to all on the road, first getting a newly married girl walking to the ration shop for kerosene, then a railway bogey inspector on leave returning to his wife after a year on the rails. Finally, at fifty he rams into the army major eagerly heading home, after ten years in a non-family station posting on the Chinese border. With most of the casualties behind him, the road is finally clear. There is only the long stretch, the black ribbon of tar, us, and the horizon. A blue highway reflecting the colour of the sky, the only bit of man-made in the sea of nothingness.

Despite the heady acceleration, the car's nautical speed reduces from a steady fifty to a shakey twenty. The metal frame lurches about in uncontrollable spasms, as if a giant mechanical arm is trying to drag it backwards. For a while no one pays heed, knowing that this is an Ambassador, a car model discarded by all leading automotive manufacturers for its inefficiency, its sluggish motion, its lack of mechanical will power, its interior designed for storage. This is the way Ambassadors have driven ever since Independence, this is the way they will continue to feel even when we are a subject nation again. Then a government clerk, carrying his wife and five children on the office bicycle overtakes us, flapping his hand in irritation towards the car's front tyre. A bullock cart does the same, the bull gazing in utter contempt at the metal version of itself. Something is wrong, clearly wrong. Even for an Ambassador. The car comes to a complete halt next to an open drain: a decision no one inside the car has made. The driver hops out of the car and announces a minor problem, a tyre puncture.

'But this is an Ambassador,' Ravi protests. 'Isn't it?'

'Sahib. Tyre is tyre.'

'But an Ambassador tyre . . .' Ravi has a point. We decide to remove the irritant altogether. The driver rolls the rubber piece down the road, and we continue. Seven hours before the Shatabdi leaves, and only twelve kilometres to the station. There is still plenty of time.

The driver reaches into his inner reserves and with one hand on the shaking steering pulls the side lever up hard: the stick rattles a bit, and after a fierce battle between the man and the machine, the car locks into cruise control. We all sit back in a dull reverie, knowing that it is technology and its appropriate applica- tion which allows man the ease and grace of a fulfilling existence. The driver leans to one side, his spine erect against the door, his right arm dangling limply outside the window, just the way driv- ers used to carrying ten passengers in front seat sit to drive—the posture of overcrowding. Like a bus commuter who sits at the edge of the seat even when there is no one else sharing it. The Gold Flake hangs out of the side of his mouth, unlit and from his expression it is easy to tell he is looking forward to discarding another part of his car so that he can buy a set of matches. A sense of vacancy and boredom has entered his eyes and is emerging through his fingertips lightly drumming the National Anthem on the steering. Further down the road, after having run over a family transporting their loved one to the electric crematorium, another grating noise erupts around us. Everyone looks about to see what it might be—a marriage party, an election rally, or a labour union leader speaking out against the management. But it is none of these things. The origin of the noise is within the car. Without stopping or slowing, the driver opens the bonnet to check. Given the speed at which we are moving this is certainly possible. He comes back and announces that the radiator has burst.

'The car still has a radiator?' Ravi asks, impressed.

'Of course Sahib,' says the driver. 'Doesn't every car have?'

'But this is an Ambassador, you know.'

'I know Sahib. It's leaking.' The driver gets emotional. 'It won't last.'

There is sadness on the driver's face, the grimness of expression is akin to that of a mother's who discovers that her child, her only son, is stricken with leukemia. And it is only a matter of days. Ravi reaches across to comfort him, saying that these things happen but life must go on. He advises the whimpering man to remove the radiator altogether.

'Altogether, Sahib?'

'Altogether,' says Ravi. 'This is an Ambassador isn't it?'

The radiator is sold to a passing junk dealer for scrap and with the extra money the driver buys himself a cigarette. The car is smooth once more. Everything is normal. Sheila resumes her vicious attack on multinationals that paint ads on the walls of national monuments. 'Did you see what Beltek TV has done to Fatehpur Sikri.'

'Did you see what Fatehpur Sikri did to Beltek.' Ravi plays devil's advocate. 'Such a beautiful site for a picture tube factory. And Akbar took the whole dammed hill.' And or what? He puffs on his pipe, 'Pachisi courts and Panch Mahal.'

'Couldn't we get Beltek to clean the walls?' Sheila's position is that of a rabid preservationist.

'I think we should get them to colour the walls they left out . . .'

I continue to stare at the road, watchful, silent.

And I begin to think of the car again. The Ambassador is like a Mont Blanc pen. It rose from the heap of European rejects in the 1950s to become the most desirable car of independent India, rising across the decades from mere national cult status to a concept. No one expects its shape to change no one expects it to ever stop running. Even when the rest of the world has given in to automotive technology, to fuel injection and water-sensory windshield wipers, even when the others look to an efficient world of speedy and comfortable transportation the Ambassador is always there, sticking its proud cream-coloured head amongst the Peugeots and Triumphs and BMWs, stating glibly: 'Look guys. Sure you'll be around for a few years, but when people realize that comfort, speed, styling, fuel efficiency, air-pollution index, colour, texture, sound, beauty are only non-essential fripperies of life, they'll be back.'

(January 1996)

ANITA ROY

Over Here

Summer is here, and flocks of expats gather in the evening sky twittering together, feeding themselves up in preparation for the long migration west. Their winter coats have been shed, and they and their young are easily distinguished by their ripe, pink summer hue. An intrepid Brit-watcher, I was privileged to observe them at close quarters at the High Commissioner's residence in New Delhi, a vital watering-hole for the species, where they annually flock in early May before the females and young prepare to undertake the difficult and taxing journey back to Surrey and Kent, leaving the males to hibernate in the isolated air-conditioned pockets of multinational offices in the city.

Armed with only my light tan camouflage and a notebook, I was able to spend time with them unobserved, without the use of a hide, thick or otherwise. Luckily my part-English parentage and BBC vowels provided me with the perfect cover, and none of the individuals either took startled flight at my appearance or mistook me for a wandering *ayah*.

We had been relieved of a few hundred bucks at the gate by a horsey woman with a bucket of cash and a penetrating stare.

'For charity, you know.'

'Of course,' we mumbled, fishing deep into our undernour-
ished handbags and pockets, 'Super.'

My friends had come prepared, armed with a rice salad. I was
tagging along, hoping that no one would notice I had brought
neither salad nor pud to add to the buffet, and send me away
empty handed and empty bellied. I found a fellow-saladless lass
who fixed me with a baleful stare and said, 'I was going to bring
a salad, but we've just had to fire our cook.' I made what I hoped
passed for a sympathetic noise and sipped my gin.

The trestle tables were dotted with bowls of pasta, trays of
sausages, quiche lorraine and baked potatoes in jolly silver foil
wrapping. The garden itself was more like an eighteen-hole
putting green, the lawn clipped to perfection. I wondered if Sir
David Gore-Booth had a *mali* who, like those in the days of the
Raj, swept the dew from the grass blades each morning so that
the sahib's trouser cuffs would not get wet. The trees were aglow
with lights—not the little star-like sprinklings that glitter at
Indian wedding parties, but huge, round tissue lampshades as
though, having trawled the night sky, they had come back with
a rich haul of full moons trapped between their twigs.

It was a perfect evening. The light rain earlier had threatened
to dampen Lady Mary's careful arrangements of origami napkins—
there's nothing like limp table linen to put a downer on the
evening—but luckily it had cleared before the guests descended,
and our serviettes were as crisp as the salad, and as stiff as our
upper lips. The wine was flowing, and the gentle chink of silver
cutlery on monogrammed china provided the background music
to the happy English chatter. We found ourselves a quiet corner
table to chow down at.

The horsey woman fetched up at our table and showed her
teeth. Her husband sat meekly by, doing his best to disappear
behind a densely wooded beard. He was clearly one of those
men for whom facial hair is a way of keeping life at bay, and he
peered from behind owlish glasses with the air of a startled faun.

'Eighteen years,' she bellowed, leaning back from him and miming surprise, 'God, darling, have we really been married that long?' The hunted look intensified a notch and he managed a weak smile before darting back behind his shrubbery.

There was a gentle ripple of applause as another extraordinarily long wedding anniversary was announced, and couples slipped each other looks ranging from affection to disbelief. Given the average age, income and physical appearance of most of the company, they tended towards the latter.

Oh, but pity the poor expat wife. 'Tis a hard road to tread and not one to be undertaken lightly. Think of the tedium, the claustrophobia of travelling from one country to another, only to be partnered in cards and clobbered at croquet by the same florid features and floral prints. 'So', I ventured, encouragingly, to the dumpy lady on my left, 'what do you do?'

'Do?' she said, blankly.

'Umm, yes, you know . . .'

There was a short pause while she flipped through the thin cardfile of her brain under *d*.

'Well, bridge.' I presumed she meant cards rather than civil engineering. 'And socials. We do a lot of those.'

Another pause, followed by a flash of inspiration.

'And of course we all do our bit for charity. That's *so* important isn't it?'

'Oh yes,' I nodded.

'I mustn't say this', she added conspiratorially, 'but Indians are the *worst* at looking after their own.'

I declined to point out that the British expat wives' contribution to the educational, social and economic reforms in the country is a mere droplet in a very Indian ocean, and that as we were sitting their exchanging pleasantries, Britain itself had just put to rout—finally—eighteen years of Tory rule in which the national health service, the welfare state and the social security system had been ritually sacrificed to the great god of 'free'

market economics and his prophet, La Thatcher. Instead I returned with renewed concentration to my quiche, while she examined a fifth glass of water for microbes.

Sir David and Lady Mary, our hosts for the evening, sailed
among their guests like galleons among a flotilla of dinghies, charm-
ing, urbane, witty and at ease, their blue blood flowing as serenely
as the English channel on a sunny August day. Instead of com-
plaining about the servants, which seemed to be the main activity
of most of the people there, Lady M arched her delicate eyebrows
and exclaimed how ridiculous to have so many staff (twenty) for
a house of this size—she gestured expansively to the sprawling
palace behind us—though she conceded that she did need a bit
of help, what with 9,000 visitors a year. There was an audible gulp,
as harried wives did a quick mental calculation. That means a
well-attended coffee every day morning for three years on the
trot. While they still work at the level of village fete, and biscuit-
tin-on-the-mantelpiece economics, her cheerful *sang froid* could
only come from years of upper-class grooming.

To the manor-born rather than toward the manor-striving
the HC and Lady M's presence threw into sharp relief the class
divisions which are the weft and warp of British social fabric.
Only in the hothouse world of Expatland will you find nice
middle-class girls from Wimbledon putting on the airs and graces
of Earls and Graces and getting away with it.

'We've got a mahv'lous *ayah* for Timmy and Louise. We're so
lucky. They simply adore her. 'Course she really runs the house.
Dam' bossy actually, but couldn't do without her. Had a lot of
problems with your servants?'

'Well, actually,' I risked admitting, 'I don't have anyone . . . er,
just at present.'

'Poor yooouu. Isn't that frightfully difficult?'

These are folks who have trotted happily down to the super-
market for years with their toddlers perched on their shopping,
gone home, vacuumed the living room, whipped up a quick

dinner, eaten it with their hubbies, watched telly, done the washing up and held down a full-time job as a marketing assistant for
years, without so much as a butler. Suddenly they're uprooted
and transplanted into tropical soil and they wilt like rain-sodden
serviettes, unable to buy a carrot from the local market without
the support of at least four domestics.

By this time of the evening, we have made short work of
the sausages and are taking the puddings in our stride. Death-by-
chocolate fudge cake, black forest gateau, blackcurrant cheese-
cakes, apple and cinnamon flan, lush trifles, lemon meringue
pie. I put all my socialist principles on the back burner and
prepared to prostrate myself before the sweet trolley. Much rolling of eyes, surreptitious loosening of belts and patting of girths.
'Oooh, I shouldn't really, but . . .' More than his fabulist prose,
more than the *Satanic Verses* controversy, more than his catapult-
ing the modern Indian novel on to the international stage, Salman
Rushdie must be congratulated for coining the slogan for the
Milk Marketing Board of Britain to advertise fresh cream cakes:
'Naughty . . . but *nice*'. These three words capture perfectly the
'oh, go on, indulge yourself; you deserve it' ethos of middle-
class, middle Englanders with their middle-aged spread and their
mid-life crises.

At this point, I was nearly rumbled. My BBC vowels, greased
along by quantities of Gilbey's Gin, had started to slip and my
carefully cultivated Anglo-Saxon mask was in danger of
following:

'Where do you live?'

'Mayur Vihar.'

'Oh! Vasant Vi . . .'

'No, *Mayur* Vihar.'

'Ah.' Blank stare. 'Where's that?'

'The other side of the river.'

'River?'

'Yes, you know the river? In Delhi? The Jamuna?'

'Oh. Oh. That river.' Pause. 'But that's *miles* away.'

'Mammm. Well, not really. I mean, I get to work in forty minutes by bus.'

'Bus?'

At this point I knew the dame was on to me. There was a long pause, her fork frozen mid air, the lemon meringue earning a brief respite on its way to meet its lip-sticky end.

'Ummm ... do you ... I mean ... is there, by any chance some, ah ... Indian blood in you?' She didn't actually say 'touch of the tar brush', but it was there, lingering in the air, the nasty taste of racism quickly subsumed beneath the sweet cloud of white meringue. I deftly turned the conversation away from my own mixed parentage and to more immediate concerns.

'Oh, I'm glad you mentioned that, because I've been wanting to find out about the expat blood donor group. Are you involved in that at all?'

'Oh yes. It's a marvellous scheme—so reassuring. You know that if you ever need blood you can just pop over to Sally's (she's called "the Vampire" ha ha ha) and she'll just ring around and get you some. You know it's really shocking but,' again lowering her voice to a conspiratorial whisper, 'they don't screen their blood.'

'Really? Don't *They?*'

Any pretence at scientific rationalist explanations for this little scheme holds little water—and even less blood—in light of the rest of the evening's conversation. It isn't HIV they're scared of. It's that (um ... ah) Indian blood which she so subtly pointed out was coursing through my adulterated veins. Perhaps she would come round from a transfusion suddenly overcome with the urge to leap on to a blueline bus, or make her own salad—my god! Who knows where it might end?

While the husbands washed down their cheesecake with Chateauneuf Du Pape, the wives shook their ample booties on the dance floor. 'That Jenny,' remarked one cigar-toting aficionado of the female form. 'God! What a body. Marvellous after three kids, eh?' The *Expat Group Newsletter* this month featured an Expat Husband's Lament which gives a rich and varied insight into the mind-set of this creature:

'Dear Heavenly Father [it starts off], try not to look down upon our disgruntled, disobedient and dishevelled Expat Wives with whom we are doomed to travel this Earth—following us through "thick and thin" as we provide for them. We are carrying out our hardworking lives in lands unknown while they are roaming and groaning about the heat and the mosquitoes and then "chicken out" by taking flight to cooler climes when they feel like it . . . Oh Great One! Give our beloved wives divine guidance in their selection of houses in totally unscheduled caste zones and in their selection of cooks to ensure that we fulfil our duties each day without getting clobbered by Delhi Belly . . . We beseech you, O Lord, to smile down on our lovely ladies and forgive them when they nag us about feeling bored out of their little female minds . . . Please Lord, control our wives each day with their impatience with the maid and try to help us to ensure that they do not thump the maid, especially if she is beautiful and we fancy her.'

With the departure of their mates and offspring to cooler climes, the remaining males hatch plans for a 'boys' weekend away' in Bangkok or Amsterdam—presumably to admire Buddhist stupas or see original Van Gogh paintings, since it wouldn't do to suggest that they might be tainting that expat blood with unscreened, un-British bodily fluids.

As the alcohol took hold, and the night drew on, the men also hitched up their tummies and took to the dance floor. There are few less edifying sights than English men trying to dance. Their gyrations and twitches were evidence enough that they wouldn't recognize rhythm if it were served up to them with watercress. The hi-fi blared out 'We gotta get out this place' and, as the stars wheeled over Rashtrapati Bhavan, this anthem of teenage rebellion was transformed into another anti-India whinge by these overfed, fed-up, nouveau Rajas and their dishevelled, bored expat Maharani-manqués. The hour was late and Mayur Vihar suddenly seemed a long way away and a far, far better place. My friends and I took the lyrics at a more mundane level, and quietly slipped away.

(June/July 1997)

Bad News

The occasional 'crime' that I covered for the *Times of India* spoiled, to a large extent, the charm of detective and crime movies for me. The calm and cultured detective was replaced by a paunchy, *paan*-chewing sub-inspector who often was in a state of obvious tension which developed into a barely subdued terror at the sight of senior officers and press teams. The careful accumulation of clues was replaced by a clear-cut confession, sometimes obtained with the help of a few choice blows in the lock-up. The only faintly recognizable thing that appeared to have permeated into the real-life world of Delhi crime from the world of detective stories was the butler—who continued to do it. But even this sinister, black-coated, bow-tied eminence had shrunk to the pitiable figure of Bihari *chokras,* the poor serving boy who had opened the door or perhaps even wielded the knife.

Crime reporting appears to be an exciting job, until one gets on the spot. Take for example the exhumation of a body, the reopening of a grave—a rather common event in detective movies and one that hardly makes our detective bat an eye. In real life, though, the stench hits you like a hammer. During the only exhumation I witnessed (in East Delhi), the body had been buried for about twelve days. It was rotting. The stench was so great that you could not stand by the grave for more than a few seconds. It made you think twice about getting buried. It stayed with you for weeks, somehow making it impossible to smell anything without that nauseating stink of death returning with full force.

Crime reporting, of course has very little to do with re-opening graves and even less with being on the spot. The thing a crime reporter needs is contacts especially in the police. His most precious possession is not acute hearing, a pen-camera or a pencil binocular, but the phone number of the sub-inspector (press). Generally referred to as SI-Press pronounced without the hyphen this sub-inspector is the tenuous link between a prying press and a mostly secretive police force. He informs you about press meets and briefings by police commissioners. He sends you news handouts. He is the first person you call to find out whether rioting has broken out in East Delhi or not. He even rings you up with details about crimes that, you can be sure, are common talk in Bengali market and elsewhere. The SI-Press is no leak: the details you get from him are generally details which the police consider not worth hiding. For details which have not yet escaped into public circulation you need to 'cultivate' various local inspectors and OICs. This is a lengthy and delicate process consisting of regular visits to police stations and jocular telephone conversations. The telephone calls go something like this:

You: Hello, hello, is Inspector Sharma there?

Gruff voice: *Round par hain, ji.*

You: Tell him Khair from the *Times of India* wants to speak to him. Urgent *hai.*

Gruffer voice: *Kah diya* na. *Round par hain.*

You: I am from the Press.

Less gruff voice: *Kaun* Press?

You: *Times of India*

Gruff voice: *Kaun?*

You: *Timej aaf In-di-aa*

Gruffer voice: *Kaun* press?

You: *Navbharat Times*

Voice: *Navbharat Times*

Voice: *Navbharat*, sir! *Ek* minute, sir! Coming sir!

This is when Inspector Sharma takes up the receiver, *hello hello hello boss,* and the two of you, *what say boss,* discuss India's latest Test match, *what first-class super knock by Tendu boss,* which is the best way to get to know a fellow Indian, *so boss drop in for chai this week boss.* With proper care and perseverence, this will give you a network of police officers who might offer you a crumb of unofficial information now and then, *or the record boss.* The *Times of India* however, appears to have a policy of reserving the slot of crime reporter for Biharis. I had been asked to fill in for the TOI's regular crimies, both friends and fellow-Biharis; the tradition, I have been told, has been continued by another Bihari. Whether this has to do with the reputation of Biharis in Delhi or the large number of Biharis in the Delhi police force remains an unsolved mystery.

Contacts are necessary not just in order to get information. They are also necessary to save your skin. It is not a pleasant feeling to have to report on a communal riot without being on a chummy standing with a dozen or so of the local police officers. It can also come in handy on other occasions.

Once when I was covering a demonstration outside the US embassy I happened to get caught on the wrong side of the barricade during a police *lathi*-charge. I had neglected to jump over to the police side of the barricade, which is the thing to do when matters start boiling over. In this case, the matter had been on the boil for sometime. The police had lobbed tear gas shells at the crowd, which had been demonstrating its support for Saddam Hussein during the first few days of Operation Desert Storm. The demonstrators, however, had grabbed the tear gas shells and lobbed them back at the police with greater success than Saddam had in countering American missile attacks. Finally, the police could take it no more and came charging, flourishing well-oiled *lathis* in a manner that made the general idea behind the charge pretty clear.

And here I was caught on the side of the crowd. That too, a dissipating crowd. I sidled my way to the outskirts of the dissolving demonstrators, hoping to keep out of policemen's view. Not an easy feat when you are six feet tall and left stranded in an open field suddenly shorn of other un-uniformed targets. Three policemen came charging at me. I flourished my press card and shouted, *Press, Press.* To no avail—upraised *lathis* were aimed at my legs. Just then another voice broke in—*Kya kar rahe ho? Press hai!* A familiar sub-inspector ran up to me, apologizing profusely. My crime contacts had paid off.

Having covered an exhumation, a couple of murders, one riot, two terrorist strikes, three or four self-immolations and *bahu-*burnings, a bloody dacoity and one case of castration in a police station, what I lost most of all—if I ever had it—was the sense of glamour attached to crime. The criminals I met were usually more illiterate, more confused and, at times, more stupid than the average person. There was no glamour in their way of life. And their victims were common people, like us, like the criminals themselves given slightly different possibilities. What one felt first of all was the futility of most of the crimes. In the beginning one also felt anger at the waste, at the senselessness of the violence. But even that was a passing phase. The day I decided not to continue in the line longer than necessary was the day I covered a dacoity in a shop in Outer Delhi. Three people, if I remember correctly, had been gunned down while they were eating *samosas.* The bodies had just been removed. The *samosas* were still lying on a low table. There was blood on the floor. And I, who had been working without food for six or seven hours, felt the waste of *samosas* more than the waste of lives that this scene signified.

(December 1996)

NARESH FERNANDES

Urban Fabric

Narayan Surve keeps the myth alive. The myth that you can make it anywhere if you can make it in Bombay.

It's also that he can't think of living anywhere else. 'I have a *relationship* with Bombay,' explains the man who is among Maharashtra's most respected poets.

As Surve runs his fingers through his greying hair, the deep furrows of six decades of life in the raw cut across his face. He takes a deep drag on his cigarette, exhales thoughtfully and searches for the right words. 'I couldn't possibly reside anywhere else', he says, 'but sometimes I can't recognize this as the city of my birth.'

Though he isn't sure exactly when he was born, Surve does know that he was abandoned in a dustbin by his natural mother. He was found and adopted by a man employed in one of the city's cotton mills. Surve worked his way through middle school and went on to find employment in the Bombay Municipal Corporation, first as a peon and later as a primary school teacher. He now runs the Pragat Pratisthan, an institution that encourages progressive Marathi literature.

Surve's poetry resonates with the thunder of the local train to Victoria Terminus, with the shouts of the head loaders in the city's docks, with the chaos of the streets. And it echoes the clatter of the looms in central Bombay's textile mills, in which Surve worked for three years from the age thirteen.

He's come a long way since, but his office—tastefully decorated with the works of young painters—isn't far from where he spent his childhood. It's on the edge of Parel, a neighbourhood its residents often refer to as Girangaon, the Village of Mills. But the Parel of Surve's boyhood isn't the Parel that he can see from his office window. Girangaon is at the vortex of Bombay's whirpool of change. As the city's real-estate prices soar ever higher and encourage mill owners to the realization that cotton textiles aren't profitable anymore, glass-and-chrome towers are springing up where factory sheds once stood. Wooden-beamed chawls—a residential arrangement for mill workers unique to Bombay— are being replaced by new office blocks. Senapati Bapat Marg, dotted with sooty chimneys, is being transformed into the city's Madison Avenue. Yuppies in floral ties now pore over television-viewership ratings in cavernous halls in which till recently white cotton fibre hung low.

For social scientists, this is a fascinating study in how economics impinges upon all else. For those in the eye of the storm, it's simply traumatic. Says Surve, 'Parel is changing. But worse, our mental landscapes are being altered too.'

To begin with, levels of unemployment have risen dramatically. Two generations ago, spinners and weavers took it for granted that their sons would find work alongside them in the mills. Not many cotton textile labourers today cling to the hope that their children will be employed here. Or anywhere else. At peak, Bombay's cotton manufacturing industry employed 2,32,326 people. In 1976, 27 per cent of Bombay's unionized labourers found work in the mills. This year 12.5 per cent of the organized workforce—80,000 people—will take home salaries from the city's fifty-four cotton mills.

The transition from a manufacturing to a service-sector economy is being hailed as a sign that Bombay is maturing along the pattern observed in cities around the globe. But mill labourers and the rest of the working class are bewildered. The service sector demands skills that they simply don't possess. Few of the new jobs created in Parel have gone to mill workers or their children. 'Do you think these people want to become advertising copywriters?' asks Meena Menon, an organizer of the Girni Kamgar Sangarsh Samiti (Committee for the Struggle of Mill Workers).

The de-industrialization of Bombay has created a pool of frustration from which fundamentalist organizations—most notably the Shiv Sena—have drawn deep. They've profited from the agony of displacement that the Left-wing Surve expressed in his poem 'Mumbai':

My father withered away toiling
so will I, and will my little ones?
Perhaps; they too face such sad nights
wrapped in coils of darkness.
My heart wells up,
seeks an outlet;
for it was my father who sculpted
your epics in stone.

The dimly lit office of the Bombay Mill Owners Association is crowded with portraits of its chairmen wearing a fascinating variety of Indian and British headgear, reflecting sartorial and political evolution over the organization's twelve-decade history. In his speech at the 120th annual general meeting last year, current chairman Hrishikesh Mafatlal made his demands clear. Bombay's mills are dying, he claimed. Mill owners should be allowed to roll down the shutters and sell the land on which their factories stand.

He didn't say anything about the stakes: 2.3 square kilometres of the 68-square kilometre island city. The mill owners could take home upward of Rs. 60,000 for each square foot.

With so much money involved, it isn't surprising that everyone wants a piece of the action. The bullets that killed Sunit Khatau, owner of Khatau Mills, laid bare the previously fuzzy links between the mill owners, Bombay's vicious underworld and the official trade union that purports to represent all the city's textile labourers. Khatau was gunned down in May 1994 as his car waited for a traffic light to turn green. His company was attempting to shift its operations to Borivili, on the outskirts of the city, and had allegedly paid off gangsters to help convince reluctant workers that the move was in their best interests. But the deal seemed to have gone awry and the gangsters turned on their patron. Textile analysts think it may be more than a mere coincidence that Sachin Ahire, general secretary of the official Rashtriya Mill Mazdoor Sangh (National Mill Workers Association), is the first cousin of notorious gang leader Arun Gawli.

But mill owners deny all links with the underworld. And they insist that they haven't turned into real-estate speculators. V.Y. Tamhane, secretary general of the Mill Owners Association, says that Bombay's textile manufacturing shops have no option but to sell out. He insists that the city's mills simply aren't viable. He says his members pay higher wages and have higher infra-structure costs than the small-scale (and unorganized) powerloom textile factories. He also has another consideration. 'We are causing massive congestion in the heart of the city,' he pleads.

It isn't easy to gauge the health of the industry from a casual reading of reports by such trade organizations as the Mill Owners Association or the Indian Cotton Manufacturers Federation. These publications are a study in paradox. Their data juxtapose high sales volumes with low profits; increasing production with shrinking employment; record growth rates with rampant sickness. The textile industry is India's biggest employer after agriculture. Last year (1995), it earned 8.3 billion dollars, accounting for nearly 30 per cent of the country's export earnings. Five of the top ten industrial houses on the *Economic Times* 500 list made their fortunes in textiles. The Tatas have sold off their mills, but the Birlas, Ambanis, Singhanias and Mafatlals retain their interests.

The textile industry also has more sick units than any other sector of India's economy.

Many workers maintain that it was the strike of 1982 that tipped Bombay's textile mills into the spiral of destruction. Called by firebrand leader Datta Samant to demand a wage increase, the agitation lasted eleven months and, technically, hasn't yet been called off. In the initial months, Samant and his Maharashtra Girni Kamgar Union (Maharashtra Mill Workers Union) inspired fanatical devotion. His demonstrations attracted hundreds of thousands of people, disgusted with their low salaries and working conditions. They were also demanding the repeal of the Bombay Industrial Relations Act, a piece of legislation from 1948 that ensures that Bombay's textile workers can only be represented by the Congress-controlled Rashtriya Mill Mazdoor Union.

But as the strike drew out, it became more difficult for the strikers to put meals on the family *thalis*. *Mangalsutras* and wedding bangles poured into the narrow shops of Girangaon's jewellers, who double up as pawn brokers. The agitation slackened when workers left Bombay to wait out the strike in their native villages, where they would be assured of food from their fields.

For the mill managements, the situation wasn't quite so tough. They used the strike as an opportunity to sell off their excess inventories, then sent yarn to be woven in the powerloom sweatshops of Bhiwandi and Malegaon. This, as it later turned out, was a fatal move. The powerloom sector has grown rapidly since then. It now produces 72 per cent of India's cloth, in contrast to the 6.4 per cent that the mill sector scrapes together.

When the strike finally petered out, the managements of ten mills chose not to reopen. Six of those resumed operations only two years ago, while four remain dormant. The Kotwal Commission, appointed by the government to report on the effects of the strike, provided these statistics: production losses were estimated at Rs 985 crores; workers lost Rs 90 crores in wages; only 1,20,000 of the 2,32,000 strikers were rehired. The commission also said that 46,575 workers hadn't been paid their dues even six years after the strike. And at least 2,600 workers died during the eleven-month agitation.

Mill owners contend that the industry hasn't yet recovered fully from the events of 1982. Tamhane says recovery hinges on the textile factories being allowed to sell the land on which they stand in order to buy modern machinery. This is a view to which the Rashtriya Mill Mazdoor Sangh firmly subscribes, says its president, Govindrao Adhik. 'How else can the owners raise such massive resources?' he asks.

But Samant's MGKU has dug in its heels. 'The builders and the government have got together to sell our city. But we won't let them,' he told a crowd that gathered at a Girangaon play-ground in April to listen to his pitch for re-election to his Lok Sabha parliamentary seat.

Samant's rhetoric went down well, as evidenced by the cheers. But he nevertheless lost the election to Shiv Sena candidate Mohan Rawle. Rawle and his party's Girni Kamgar Sena (the Mill Work-ers Army) also have promised to stall all further sales of mill land. And Menon's Girni Kamgar Sangarsh Samiti has taken to block-ading mills that owners are attempting to clear of machinery. Said activist Balkrishna Nar, as he and other agitators stopped trucks from carting carding machines out of Piramal Mills at the end of May, 'We don't want voluntary retirement packages. We want to keep our jobs.'

To many, Bombay's hopes of regenerating itself lie in Parel. 'This is the opportunity for the city to avoid urban disaster,' says Rahul Mehrotra of the Urban Design Research Institute think-tank. He believes cheap housing and parks can be built in Girangaon.

Seemingly with a view to fulfilling these very objectives, the Maharashtra government in 1991 revised its Development

Control Regulations to allow mills to sell their land if the units are sick or want to modernize. Mill owners who sell land must surrender one-third of the area for parks and playgrounds, while another third will be reserved for public housing. There is, however, a loophole: these provisions don't apply if the mill decided to sell less than 15 per cent of its total area. That's allowed seventeen mills to begin construction projects so far without any land reverting to the city.

The state government, clearly, is of the opinion that Bombay's mills are obsolete. For the officials, it's only a question of negotiating the best possible redundancy packages for the workers. Explains Neela Satyanarayanan, Maharashtra's textile secretary, 'History marches on. We have to consider whether this land is being used in the most economical manner.'

The mill lands play a vital role in the plan drawn up by Bombay First, a foundation funded by private industry, to develop the city into a global financial centre. The foundation believes that Bombay's geographical location offers it the advantage of being able to do business with when Tokyo is asleep, but London and New York are abuzz with activity.

This would, of course, accelerate the growth of Bombay's service sector. But even government planners warn that such a trend could be disastrous. The Bombay Metropolitan Regional Development Authority blueprint for the city over the next two decades says that continuing industrial stagnation could send its economy into a tailspin, resulting in serious social unrest. The BMRDA planners point out that the city of London had to introduce massive rejuvenation programmes after jobs in the manufacturing sector dropped by more than 50 per cent in two decades, to 580,000 in 1983 from 1.4 million in 1961. Ironically, Bombay First is modelled on a similar British organization called London First. Says Arvind Adarkar, an architect involved with the Nivara Hakk Samiti housing rights organization, 'It's so stupid. Why do we have to make the same mistakes that they did?'

The foundation of Bombay's much-vaunted cosmopolitan culture was consolidated in Girangaon in the mid-nineteenth century. Many of the early textile workers were drawn from Maharashtra's lush Konkan coastal strip (so much so that many of those districts developed into money-order economies, dependent largely on remittances from relatives in the metropolis). But in a break with traditional caste-determined occupational patterns, Marathas and Kunbis worked alongside Bhaiyyas from Uttar Pradesh, Padmashali weavers from Andhra Pradesh and people from just about every part of the subcontinent. They expressed their desire to forget customary stratifications to forge a better future when, in 1881, they formed India's first trade union, the Bombay Mill Hands Association.

That idealism spilled out of the factories after they finished their shifts and went home to the same sprawl of chawls. Many of these now-crumbling extended-family dwelling units sprang up in the 1920s, when the Bombay Development Directorate took it upon itself to provide comprehensive industrial housing for 50,000 workers. In the end, the agency only managed to build 16,000 rooms because 'the people for whom they were being provided refused to occupy them until thousands of rupees had been spent modifying them into something remotely fit for human habitation,' wrote architect Claude Bartley.

The improvements, such as they were, were rudimentary at best. Consider this description of the average chawl dwelling from Kiran Nagarkar's novel, *Ravan and Eddie*: 'Each room was 12 feet wide and 24 feet deep with a wide wooden partition separating the drawing room-cum-study, library, playpen or whatever from the kitchen, which doubled as a dining room and bathroom (a tiny four-foot washing space with a tap was cordoned off on one side with a two-foot wall on which were stacked pots of water).'

In the seven decades since they were built, the claustrophobia of the chawls and the absolute lack of privacy they afford have fostered institutions that emphasize community above all else. In Worli's BDD chawls, in Sewri and in Naigaon, the rhythms of life duplicate themselves. In dingy *vyayamshalas*, teenage boys pump iron under posters of Sunil Shetty, Shivaji and Schwarzenegger. Bhajan mandals are the perfect way for the enthusiastic and the unmelodic to seek the truth. Festivals are celebrated across community boundaries with the same vigour. In fact, when Lokmanya Tilak devised the Ganesh Chaturti festival just over hundred years ago as a means of encouraging a nationalistic spirit, he chose to hold the first celebrations in a Parel chawl. The Elephant God has since become Bombay's patron deity.

Girangaon also saw the flowering of a subaltern poetry and *shair* tradition. 'Talented people like Daya Pawar, Shahir Sable, Annabhau Sathe and Shahir Amar Shaikh lived here and found inspiration here,' says Neera Adarkar, an activist of the Girangaon Bachao Andolan or Save Girangaon Movement. Her organization has put together poetry readings and music concerts attempting to show Bombay, how much less vibrant it will become with the physical destruction of Parel. Says Gajanan Khatu, another supporter of the organization, 'The kind of cultural activity here is unique. It's a blend of forms from across the country.'

But it's evident that the battle is quickly slipping from their grasp. Though Bombay's population has grown over the decade, BMRDA statistics show that Girangaon actually has fewer residents. That's evident in Nare Park Municipal School, on the edge of a maidan that was the venue for massive rallies during the Samyukta Maharashtra movement in 1956 and during the 1982 textile strike. As in the case with several other lower schools across the island city, the authorities can't find enough students to fill the benches. So they've allowed a non-governmental organization to set up its offices on the top floor.

The unemployed are moving back to their villages, while others have dispersed to larger tenements in the suburbs. With the wave of migration, the poets have turned to writing television scripts and many theatre groups have been disbanded. When the bulldozers moved in on Lalbaugh's Hanuman Theatre in April, they seemed to destroy much more than only the last performance space in Bombay for the robust song-and-dance *tamasha* form. Narayan Surve, the Parel poet, has observed the disintegration from up close. 'There's no cohesive culture anymore, just a few remaining stands of custom and tradition,' he sighs.

More than a century after the great cotton boom, few Bombay residents remember that it was the White Gold that allowed the city's best-known stone epics to be built. And few are conscious of how the fibre has woven itself into the names by which they know their neighbourhoods. The most obvious nomenclatural indicator of the time cotton was king is, of course, Cotton Green. The Green has long been built over with boxy warehouses in which fewer cotton bales are stacked with each passing year. A million Bombay office workers stop at Cotton Green for thirty seconds each day as their trains travel on to the commercial district beyond Victoria Terminus, but few hear history's whispers.

Just as the worshippers on their way to pay homage to the vermilion-faced goddess from whom the city may derive its name are deaf to the past when they ask the bus driver to let them off at the Cotton Exchange stop. Paint peeling off its stone facade, the building that once was the hub of Bombay's economy is now simply a convenient landmark to help the disoriented find Mumbadevi temple.

And almost no one discerns the hum of the spinning rotor in the chimes of the Rajabai clock tower that float out over the Oval Maidan every half hour. The magnificent Porbunder-stone tower was built by Premchand Roychand in memory of his mother. Roychand made his pile during the cotton explosion of the 1860s, when the American Civil War forced Manchester to buy massive stocks from the subcontinent. Prices on the Bombay

Green leapt from Rs 180 a kandy to Rs 700 and exports more than doubled from Rs 16 crores to Rs 40 crores in the five years that the bubble lasted. The city earned approximately eighty-one million pounds sterling during that period and Roychand displayed the sort of acumen that would come to be associated with Harshad Mehta more than a century later. Roychand wangled his way into becoming a major shareholder in the Bank of Bombay and worked out schemes to withdraw Rs 1.38 crores. He added to his fortune by obtaining a little in advance of his Bombay competitors the London cotton prices that determined local trends, dispatching smaller country boats to waylay mail ships by the lighthouse off Bombay harbour.

When the crash came with the end of the Civil War, the bank had to write off a full 40 per cent of his advances.

By then, Bombay's first cotton textile mill had already been coughing out black smoke for eleven years. The Bombay Spinning and Weaving Company had been started in 1854 by a Parsi merchant named Cowasjee Nanabhoy Davar for the avowed purpose of fighting Manchester 'with her own weapons'. When it became apparent that he had a good thing going with cheap labour, easily available raw material and a large local market, Davar opened the city's second mill, four years later. By 1865, Bombay's skyline was dotted with ten chimneys. The mills had 25,000 spindles and 3,400 looms, processed 40,000 bales of cotton every year, and employed 6,000 people.

Poet Namdeo Dhasal says that even though he can't quite comprehend Girangaon's metamorphosis over the last three decades, he thinks the changes are vastly desirable. 'The old methods of production have become obsolete,' he says. 'That's the imperative of progress.'

In 1972, he was among the founders of the radical lower caste Dalit Panther movement. Now a greying forty-eight-year-old, he continues to be involved in politics, as a member of the fragmented and fractious Republican Party of India. Across from the rugby field of the exclusive Bombay Gymkhana, Dhasal holds court most afternoons in an asbestos-roofed cramped shed that serves as the headquarters of the Gavai faction to which he now is aligned.

Last month, he took on Congress bigwig Suresh Kalmadi in parliamentary elections in Pune. He lost his deposit, but doesn't seem to bothered. Speak of the changes that are sweeping Bombay, however, and he becomes instantly animated. 'Bombay is my oxygen, my blood. I can't live without it,' he declares, his steel-rimmed reading glasses riding low on his forehead. Dhasal says he's perturbed by the fact that the culture of the working classes is being replaced by 'imperialist culture, the worst possible exports from the west'.

But he seems to be riding out the turbulence rather grace-fully. Like thousands of others, he's moved out to a more salu-brious neighbourhood. He occasionally visits his old home, on the fringes of the city's red-light district, in his white Toy-ota Cerrida with windows that roll down automatically. Bombay, it would seem, is his oyster. Or perhaps, to use his own metaphor, his strumpet. That's what he says in 'Bombay, My Beloved Whore':

> You be faithful to us
> You warm up our beds
> Play the flute of Eternity
> Play around with our dreams
> Breathe fire into our sperms
> O footloose hussy
> O churlish slut
> O Khandoba's concubine
> O wanton coquette
> O whore with the heart of gold
> I won't go away from you like a ragged beggar

I'll strip you to the bone
Come, throw open the gates of heaven to the poor devils
Bombay, my beloved whore
I'll take you for a ride
I'll strike you dumb
And go.

(July 1996)

MANJULA PADMANABHAN

Transports of Delight

In the jungle of urban traffic, it is the bumble bee. Buzzing in
and out of lanes, squeezing between Marutis and Redline
buses, cheeking Tata trucks and challenging the laws of physics,
the Three-wheeled Scooter Rickshaw (TSR) of Indian city
streets is an example of Survival of the Unfittest.

A gas trap for poisonous fumes, unstable and flimsy, it is probably the most dangerous vehicle in which to negotiate our blood-
stained streets. If its seat is padded then the passenger sits too high
and is in danger of being brained by the overhead struts holding up
the canopy. If the seat is unpadded, then every bump and rut and
pot-hole registers as hammer blows to the passenger's fragile sinews.

I know at least one person who has a permanent back problem
because she sneezed just as her auto, having been flung into orbit
by a speed-breaker, impacted the planet once more. Another friend
was hurled out and suffered near-fatal injuries to his head when
his chariot took a corner at Grand Prix speeds. Yet another was in
a vehicle which toppled over on its side, causing her to slide out,
according to her, 'as neatly as a loaf of bread from an oven!'

And yet the little motorized disasters thrive!

In part, the secret of their success is that they occupy a niche
which serves travellers who cannot afford the flea-infested

solitude of a taxi's seat yet are fastidious enough to disdain the sweaty intimacies offered by a bus. Just like an insect species, TSRs are too small to attract competition from the larger entities on the road, but they make up in numbers what they lack in volume.

The helmsman at the controls of a TSR is a singular individual. Though we have reports from *Outlook* magazine that women autorickshaw drivers are flourishing in Kerala, here in the wilds of the North, it is hard to imagine such a development. The other drivers would probably rise up in revolt at the mere suggestion of women puttering the streets alongside them. Local rickshaw stands have the appearance of being impromptu club-houses for young men, thin as animated string beans, their eyes glazed over from staring into a better future.

Perhaps the reason they are generally very young is that they don't survive for long enough to mature at their vocation. Despite their youth they are unusually disgruntled and cantankerous. One rarely sees them smiling or kidding about. When a potential passenger approaches the stand, the team of waiting drivers stirs uneasily, warily, as if tensed for attack.

The likelihood of finding a driver willing to travel towards the destination of one's choice varies in inverse proportion to the climate and the desperation of one's need. The hotter it is and the greater the load of parcels one bears, the less chance once has of being accommodated on the seat of a TSR. The driver will not be budged by entreaties, histrionics or threats. He makes it clear that if he conveys you hither and yon, it is purely at his whim.

In Madras, TSR drivers consider it their privilege to extort a higher price than whatever the meter shows, giving no reason other than their superior desire in the face of one's reluctance. In Bombay, rickshaw drivers have the example of Bombay's excellent cabbies to contend with and are therefore abnormally civil and honest. But in Delhi, the TSR driver considers it his duty to keep the local citizenry on its collective toes. No opportunity to take longer routes is let slip. No momentary lack of small change is left unexploited.

Once, when I caught my charioteer going twice the distance he need have, he shrugged, grinned and reset his meter without argument: No problem! he seemed to say, I'm a rascal and I know it!

But one can grow indulgent of their ill-tempered little ways. Their existence is a bone-rattling tedium of hauling human cargo from one end of the city to the next, while they themselves seem to be on a one-way street to nowhere. And though they are usually taciturn, they speak volumes in the ways that they outfit their three-wheeled batter-buggies.

Some drivers swaddle the front and rear wheelguards with webs of metal tubes, while others content themselves with disco brakelights. Some have pennants and flags hanging from the rear-view mirrors, others have foxtails and long-haired baby-dolls dangling inside, down the centre of the windscreen. Delhi's autos prevent access from the right side of the passenger seating area, which is sometimes sealed over and fitted with a metal flap, like a travelling *zenana*. In Madras and Bangalore, autos are smart and sturdy, their paintwork bright and their upholstery shiny. In Bombay, where TSRs cannot ply further south than Bandra, they often sport sophisticated electronic equipment and will play a selection of the latest film hits on request.

While the vehicles of other metros have a reverse gear, Delhi's autos can only move forward. I asked a driver why this was so and he said that the drivers consider the gear an unnecessary luxury. So they remove it and sell it to spare-parts dealers.

There is a lively tradition of rickshaw art, with Madras leading the pack for sheer virtuosity. Perhaps the famous hoarding painters fill their spare time with commissions to decorate the rear ends of autos with gaudy sunsets, towering mountain peaks and lurid political symbols.

Delhi's rickshaw owners seem to prefer verbal messages. There are those with Urdu verses painted onto the rear, such as this, the most elaborate one I've seen: *Phool maine dhekha, gulab jaise nahin. Shair maine suna, Mirza Ghalib jaise nahin.* More commonly, there are passionate avowals of ownership: *Bunti di gaddi!* Various shades of love are a favourite theme for dorsal epigrams. There are solemn declarations of devotion to the Mother (*Maa ki amanat*) while romantic love is viewed with frank alarm: 'Love is Sweet Poison' appears with dismaying frequency. There are more robust souls, however, because I have also seen a message which reads: 'Love For Sale—100% discount'.

There are standard ornaments in the form of 3D reliefs showing the canonical slinky-eyed village belle squinting with seductive purpose at the bumpers of other conveyances. There are plastic-pink Ganeshas, jaunty tridents, multi-coloured Oms, the Islamic three-letter formula which looks vaguely like the English alphabets 'LAY', the crossed swords of the Sikhs and even a crucifix or two. No Buddhas, Mahavirs or Zoroasters, however!

There are cat's eye reflectors winking at the rear-view observer. And evil-eye deflectors in the form of dangling slippers and devil faces. There are stylized birds and bleeding hearts pierced with arrows the size of javelins—a reference, no doubt, to the fatal side-effects of love.

Tweeters have peevishly squawking electric horns and Woofers have hand-powered klaxons blatting like crack-voiced adolescent boys. There are the yellow-canopied jalopies and the black-canopied ones. There are the open-to-the-elements wallahs and the double-layer-of-waterproofing wallahs. There are designer interiors with tiger strips painted onto the inner surface of the canopy. There are pin-up girl specials with fleshy meteorettes from the film industry leering from the walls. There are minibordellos, with chintz curtains and mirrors on the partition, so that one is menaced by reflections of traffic forever bearing down upon one.

With so much invention and creativity on view, it may seem a waste of time to offer suggestions for further evolution. But every thriving niche attracts its would-be improvers and extenders. Here, then, is a brief survey of the possibilities awaiting the adventurous auto-designer.

Bikaneri Phut-Phut

One of a series of architecturally inspired TSRs, the Bikaneri is an example of the cultural challenge awaiting the tourist trade. By creating TSRs that reflect the ethos of different regions of India, they advertise crafts and aesthetics while providing employment to the natives of each area. Drivers are chosen from the language group specific to each architectural style. Where possible, their uniforms reflect their community. Ideally, they are trained to act as impromptu guides and are able to speak knowledgeably about their places of origin. Each vehicle is individually con-structed and all repairs are borne by the relevant State governments.

Autorustic

For that bucolic touch. Operates just like a bullock-cart, without the nuisance of bullocks! Large wheels facilitate deep ruts and fathomless pot-holes. Generous seating area allows for the transmigration of whole families from one locality to the other. The rear of each vehicle is hand-made from purely vegetarian, one hundred per cent biodegradable materials. Accessories include authentic wood splinters and live cattle-ticks. It is
expected to win
many prizes at
trade fairs for
environment-
friendly
technolo-
gies.

God's Rocket

A compact temple-to-go. Scaled-down versions of all the leading places of worship, with models for the devout of every faith. Recordings of devotional songs played for the duration of the journey. The driver is an ordained priest and is sanctioned to perform all or any ceremonies required of him en route. While the chief among these, given the conditions on our roads, are last rites, he must be prepared to perform marriages, births and name-givings as well. Depending on his inclination he is authorized to settle disputes and to offer philosophical advice. In rare cases, following the famous classical precedent, he may even advise a royal passenger to go forward into battle.

Baroque-on-Wheels

A little something for those who like to showcase their taste for ostentation. Male and female cherubs available on demand. Also: garden gnomes, Bambis, Easter bunnies, Dennis the Menace, rearing stallions and that perennial favourite, the incontinent little boy called Manneken-Pis borrowed from the fountains of Brussels. All available in a range of metallic colours including gold, silver and radium. Seats covered in Seizure Blue brocade. Frescoes painted on the ceiling. And twelve-tune musical horns.

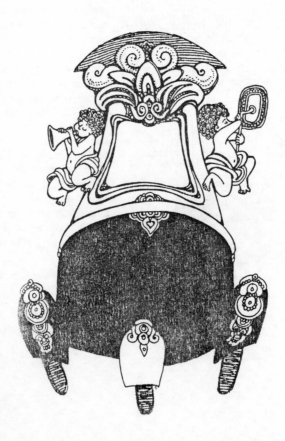

Hell's Trishaw

This is an eye-catching model, guaranteed to cause maximum stress in fellow motorists. Fashion accessories for drivers include safety-pin earrings and stick-on scars. Ideal for road-hogs, minor traffic offenders and psychotics alike, this handy little vehicle can be ordered with a choice of lethal weapons. Not recommended for the family man.

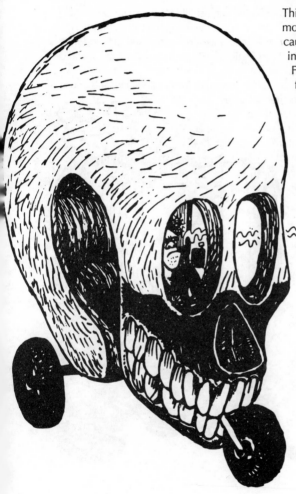

Auto-Ethnotic

This elegant machine was created exclusively for the mansion owner who yearns for tastefully appointed vehicles to convey her/him from room to room within the residence. Ingeniously devised to blend in with ethno-chic salons, each vehicle is customized to suit the specific decor of the customer.

When not in use, the unit can be converted into an attractive and unusual armchair. Components are crafted by authentic masters of ancient automotive traditions of the nation. Canopies are available in a limited edition of weaves and embroideries. Matching outfits for the ladies of the house can be ordered separately, tailoring charges extra.

Strato-Darter

This sleek model can be used in any sector of the galaxy. It is of great use during traffic jams and at rush hours. It can officially accommodate four passengers at a time, but in practice many more have been accommodated. The Darter reaches warp speeds of ten and above, having raced against the USS Enterprise of *Star Trek* in its time—which, unfortunately is a few centuries away yet.

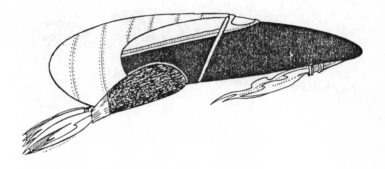

Road Rani

For the driver who cannot bear to dawdle, a TSR which leaves the Zens and the Contessas far behind.

Low-slung, fast and furious, the Road Rani is a marvel of engineering, combining the homespun construction of a traditional rickshaw with the agility of a Formula One racer. Passengers travel at their own risk and must be warned of hazards which include a whiplash at traffic lights and accidental ejection.

(April 1996)

Notes on Contributors

Amit Chaudhuri was educated in Bombay and at University College, London, and took a doctorate in English from Balliol College, Oxford. He was Creative Arts Fellow at Wolfson College, Oxford, and Leverhulme Fellow at the Faculty of English, Cambridge. He has published four novels, the latest of which is *A New World*. He has won the Betty Trask Award, the Commonwealth Writers Prize, the Encore Prize, the Southern Arts Literature Prize, and, most recently, the Los Angeles Times Book Prize for Fiction.

Amita Baviskar teaches at the Department of Sociology, University of Delhi. Her research centres around the sociology of environment and development. She is the author of *In the Belly of the River: Tribal Conflicts over Development in the Narmada Valley* (Oxford University Press 1995).

Anita Roy returned to India in 1996, having lived most of her life in England, to work as an academic commissioning editor for Oxford University Press in Delhi. She reviews regularly for British and Indian newspapers and magazines, and is a regular columnist for *Man's World*. Her interests in the blurry bit where East meets West are perhaps explained by her being a bit of a hybrid herself.

Bishakha Datta is one of the founders of Point of View, a non-profit organization in Bombay that promotes the point of view of women through a creative use of media. A journalist by training, Bishakha makes documentary videos, writes articles, essays and books, and does consultancies for development organizations. Her aim in life is to work less, holiday more and indulge her dreams.

Gautam Bhatia is a Delhi-based architect.

Kai Friese edited the *India Magazine* from 1995 until 1998. He is currently Features Editor of *Man's World* magazine.

Latha Anantharaman is a writer, editor and translator. She wrote this article when she was assistant editor at the *India Magazine*.

Manjula Padmanabhan (b: 1953) is a writer and artist living in New Delhi. She has illustrated twenty-one books for children. Her cartoon strip SUKI appeared daily in the *Pioneer* for six years. *Hot Death, Cold Soup*, a collection of short stories, has been published in India, the UK, Holland and Italy. Her fifth play, *Harvest* won the 1997 Onassis Award for Theatre and is currently being filmed by Govind Nihalani. Her first book, *Getting There*, published by Picador India, is scheduled for release in September 2000.

Mukul Kesavan published a novel, *Looking Through Glass* in 1995. He helps edit *Civil Lines*, an occasional literary miscellany and teaches history at Jamia Millia Islamia, New Delhi.

Naresh Fernandes has been a reporter for the *Times of India* and the Associated Press in Bombay. His pieces have appeared in *Biblio*, *Man's World*, the *Chicago Tribune*, the *Los Angeles Times* and *Transition*, among other publications. He now lives in Brooklyn, New York, and works on the overseas desk of the *Wall Street Journal*.

Palagummi Sainath is a freelance journalist, based in Mumbai. After taking an MA in History from Jawaharlal Nehru University, he joined the United News of India in 1980. Later he became foreign editor of the *Daily* and deputy chief editor of the weekly *Blitz* in Mumbai. In early 1993, he left *Blitz* to work full-time on rural poverty, after winning a *Times of India* Fellowship to pursue the subject. His work in that area won him a further twelve awards and fellowships over the next two years including the prestigious European Commission's Journalism Award, the Lorenzo Natali Prize, and the PUCL Human Rights Journalism Award.

Pankaj Mishra was born in Jhansi and and grew up in small towns across north and central India. In 1992, he moved to Mashobra, Himachal Pradesh, and has been a full time writer since. He has published essays and reviews in the *Indian Review of Books*, the *Times Literary Supplement*, the *New York Review of Books*, the *New York Times*, the *Washington Post*, and the *New Statesman* among others. He is the author of *Butter Chicken in Ludhiana* and *The Romantics*.

Peter Hanley is an independent writer and a sculptor in lost-wax bronze. He lives in Delhi.

Ruchir Joshi is a writer and filmmaker. Among the films he has made are Eleven Miles, a feature-length documentary on the Bauls of Bengal, Tales from Planet Kolkata, a film essay satirising western perceptions of Calcutta, Memories of Milk City, a short film on fast-food and modernity in Ahmedabad, and Dream before Wicket, a documentary on cricket fever in Bombay and Calcutta. During the 80s, Joshi wrote regularly as a film and theatre critic for the *Telegraph*, Calcutta. Most recently, he contributed regularly to *India Magazine* before its sad and premature demise. His first novel, *The Last Jet-Engine Laugh*, will be published later this year by IndiaInk in India, and in early 2001 by Flamingo in the UK.

Shuddhabrata Sengupta is a writer and documentary filmmaker who works with the Raqs Media Collective in New Delhi. He lives between two computers and several e-mail IDs, hangs around in bus stops, and airports in real life, and in science-fiction web-sites on the internet. He hopes someday to learn cooking, Persian and web design.

Siddhartha Deb grew up in a small town in North-East India. He went to college and university in Calcutta and has worked as a journalist for national publications in Calcutta and Delhi. He now lives in New

York City and is working on a Ph.D in English Literature from Columbia University. He has just finished his first novel.

Sohaila Abdulali is the author of the bestselling novel *The Madwoman of Jogare* and three children's books. She divides her time between New York and India. She has just finished her second novel and started work on a book about the Adivasis of Maharashtra.

Sonia Jabbar is an independent writer currently living and researching in Kashmir.

Suketu Mehta is currently writing a non-fiction book about Bombay, to be published in 2001, and a novel. He is a winner of the Whiting Writers' Award, an O. Henry Prize for his fiction, and a New York Foundation for the Arts Fellowship. His articles and stories have been published in *Harper's Magazine*, *Granta*, *Time Magazine*, and the *Village Voice*. He lives in New York and Bombay.

Tabish Khair was born in Bihar and worked for the *Times of India* in Gaya and Delhi. He obtained a doctorate from Copenhagen University, where he currently teaches English. He is the author of *Where Parallel Lines Meet* (Penguin) and three other collections of poems, a novel and a book of criticism (Babu Fictions) forthcoming from OUP.